I0697255

Anxiety,

Depression,

OCD and Me

By Elizabeth Evans

This book is dedicated to my family and friends, without whom I would not have made it this far.

This book is also dedicated to everyone out there struggling with mental illness— you are not alone.

TABLE OF CONTENTS

Trigger Warning: This book contains topics pertaining to mental health that may be triggering to some readers. Please only read this book if you are in the mental space to do so. This story can wait until you are in the proper mind space to read it. This is NOT a mental health guide— this is a recounting of experiences from my life. If you are feeling like you may harm yourself or others, please seek emergency medical help.

Chapter 1

Real Life

There are so many reasons I hate having OCD that I could probably spend the rest of my life making a list of them. And I know I'll never be able to truly encapsulate the effects it's had on my life and put them on paper; but I figure I might as well try.

A lot of people have the misconception that OCD is all about things being neat and clean all the time. While that may be true for some people with OCD, that's not necessarily the case for others. OCD is specific to every individual, and there is a broad spectrum of fears that it could focus on. For some people, the fear could be coming into contact with a specific animal or hearing a certain word. For others it could be getting contaminated by germs or not having everything "just right". OCD takes that fear, which becomes an obsession, and offers one very specific escape from all of the anxiety that obsessing over the fear brings: a ritual. Rituals also vary from situation to situation and have different degrees of importance. For example, I have hundreds of dissimilar rituals for specific situations, all different in the urgency with which they must be done.

What Obsessive Compulsive Disorder does, is it takes one of your greatest fears and uses it against you. Whatever it is, you start obsessing over it. And I'm not just saying that you think about it every now and then, and you get a little freaked out. *Every* second of your life you are consumed with a fear that you may very well be aware is irrational, but that doesn't take any of the anxiety away. And the anxiety isn't just a little panic– it's the type of pure terror that gives you panic attacks that leave you unable to breathe or move or talk. Over time, you adopt "rituals" or compulsions to lessen the fear and get that ever-present voice out of your head. And suddenly you're extremely aware of how certain things could affect your life even though they have nothing to do with you.

Something that most people who do not suffer from OCD don't know is that more often than not, we, people with OCD, know that the thoughts and rituals are irrational. The anxiety could be about something that is so petty in daily life that no one else gives it a second thought. But our worlds revolve around it. We usually know that the fear is unreasonable, and we know that the rituals won't stop what we're worried about from happening; but that doesn't make the distress any less real.

This can all get pretty confusing, so I'll give you a hypothetical situation. Let's say you have OCD focused on the worry of something happening to your parents, and you constantly think about every possible thing that could happen to them. You visualize every situation, obsessing to the point that your daily life is impaired– you can't get anything done because all you can focus on are possible dangers to your parents. The only relief is completing the ritual of finding the nearest doorknob and turning it three times to the right. As if somehow, this prevents something from happening to the people you care about.

So you do it. And the anxiety automatically becomes less intense. From then on, whenever you get that specific thought about your parents being harmed, you rush to find the nearest doorknob and turn it three times to the right. Over time, though, it becomes the rule that you have to turn *every doorknob in your house* three times to the right before you leave for work in the morning *in addition to* twisting the *nearest* doorknob when the troublesome thought pops up, or else something will happen to your parents. Then after a few weeks, it becomes the rule that you have to turn *every doorknob you see* three times to the right no matter where you are, *and* you have to turn every knob in your house three times before you leave for work in the morning, *and* you have to twist the nearest doorknob when that specific thought pops up, or else something will happen to your parents. And it just keeps snowballing from there.

Basically, what OCD does is it gives you rituals to try to prevent the thing you're scared of from happening. The rituals eventually become a part of your daily life, your day revolves around them, and it seems perfectly normal to you. The worst part, though, is that soon you have so many rituals that it feels like you're trapped inside the confines of your brain, and any hope for freedom is gone.

I've struggled with mental illness for more than half of my life. And– I'm not going to sugar coat it– it sucks. Almost every stage of my life has been marked by a gain or loss of certain rituals, a change in medication, or a new origin of fear that has to be addressed in order for me to function on a day-to-day basis.

And my entire experience isn't even completely out of the ordinary. In fact, it's common to struggle with mental health issues. People all over the world struggle with OCD, anxiety, and depression, and each case is unique to them, while at the same time sharing a few of the same characteristics as other cases. A lot of people have gone through something similar to what I've gone through, but no one will ever know every single thing that I've dealt with over the years. The same goes for everyone else with mental illness.

My point is people go through this stuff every day. People all around you could be struggling with the same things I did and still do, but you may never know. If they're anything like me they've gotten good at hiding it. Because the truth is, usually the people with the most severe cases of mental illness don't talk about it with other people. Instead, we try to live our lives the way neurotypical people do, which doesn't involve openly discussing mental health issues. We know that it's not a fashion trend or something that we can use to get us out of deadlines and obligations. We know that's not how it works. It runs much deeper than that.

While the details of what I've gone through are specific to me, people struggle with this all around you. And you may never know, because a lot of people will suffer silently. So, no, I'm not special for having mental health issues. A lot of people do. By writing this book I'm not trying to show that I'm different from everyone else. I'm simply trying to use what I've gone through as an example to show that mental illness is not only real, but it's also way more common than a lot of people realize.

I also want to make it very clear before we move on that by writing this, I'm not trying to gain anyone's sympathy. Everyone is entitled to their own opinions about the reality of mental illness. All I ask is that your opinion is an informed one. My main goal for writing this is to illustrate to people *without* mental illnesses what it is like to have one… or several. My other goal for writing this is to show people who *are* struggling with what I went through and am continuing to go through that they are not alone. More people struggle with mental illness than we realize, and it doesn't make us "crazy" or "touched". If anything, it makes us more human.

So, here's my story exactly as I remember it. I hope it will shed some light on what living with a mental illness is really like. And to anyone who has gone through or is currently going through this– you're not alone.

Chapter 2

How it All Began

I don't really remember much of my childhood. I guess I remember what an average person could up until about first grade, but after that there's almost nothing. I've been told that my inability to remember the majority of second through seventh grades may have something to do with my OCD or something to do with my medication I'm taking to control it. Given the fact that I can't remember large portions of that period, I will explain this the best I can, because this is where it all started.

I was six, and Baby-Me was nothing if not a rule follower. I had always been incredibly eager to learn– a typical goody-good, straight A student. I never did anything to get in trouble; I loved school and I loved the teachers. That year, I was starting the second grade, and I was so sure it was going to be *my* year. That's when our class finally became big kids– we got to play in the big yard and do homework and everything. I was excited, and everyone in my family knew it.

Then I got sick; I came down with a fever during the first week of the December of my second-grade year. My parents didn't think much of it, obviously, because kids get sick all the time, especially in winter during the school year. No big deal. I was out of school for about a week with a fever, but I was well enough to go back pretty quickly.

But I didn't. The first three days of the next week I simply refused to go to school, even though I was feeling better. I couldn't say why, but I had developed an overwhelming fear about something happening to my mom while I was gone. I wanted to stay home to prevent anything bad from happening to her. I never wanted to leave her side, and any time we were separated, no matter how short, I became extremely anxious.

My parents were concerned, but when they asked if they should be truly alarmed, they were told that I just had "mommy-itis" after being sick at home for a week. And after those three days refusing to let my mom out of my sight, I seemed to calm down a little; I was able to start going to school again. It looked like that bout of anxiety had passed, and I was feeling much better.

Then, one evening, my mom got a call from my teacher, Mrs. G, informing her that something was wrong. Mrs. G told my mom that after she handed me my test that day, I had just sat there in my chair without starting it. This was completely different from what I would have usually done, and Mrs. G knew it. She told my mom that she had walked over to non-test-taking me and asked what was wrong.

To her surprise, instead of answering her question I asked, "What am I supposed to do?" She reminded me to simply put my name at the top of the paper and begin the test. After printing my name on the top of the page I looked at her again.

"What do I do now?"

Mrs. G told my mom that was when she knew there was something really wrong with me. I was the six-year-old who rarely asked questions and always took tests willingly. And suddenly I didn't know what to do after writing my name. For my parents, that was the first red flag.

The next one came not long after that, when my mom found me standing at the top of the staircase crying. When she asked me what was wrong, I told her that I didn't know how to get down the stairs, even though I had never had a problem with stairs in the past. My mom had to guide me down the steps, because suddenly I couldn't do it alone. I had lived in a house with stairs all my life, and this uneasiness made my parents very aware of my recent weird behaviors.

The only reason I could give for this sudden change was that I felt like something bad would happen if I went down the stairs. The feeling was so overwhelming that I felt stuck upstairs, and I was worried that I would never be able to get back down. The only way I felt I would be safe from my unknown threat was if my mom accompanied me.

A few weeks after that, my mom found me crying again, this time at the bottom of the stairs. I was facing two hallways that went in separate directions but wrapped around the house to lead to the same place. After calming me down a little, my mom asked what the problem was, and I responded, "I don't know which way to go." That trivial decision was my dilemma: I couldn't figure out which hallway to take to get to the kitchen.

Both hallways led to the same place, and it took approximately the same amount of steps whichever hallway I chose. It really wasn't a big deal. But something in my head was making it almost impossible for me to make the choice myself. I couldn't put my finger on it or put it into words, but I felt like something bad would happen if I chose the first hallway. And when I went to take the second hallway I got the same feeling. So I just sat down and cried, because I didn't know what else to do.

On another occasion, I had a mini mental breakdown because I couldn't figure out which side of the washcloth to put the soap on. Again, the problem was completely illogical. I felt that using either side would have harmful results for a reason I couldn't explain. My parents didn't need any more proof after that to know that something was really wrong with me, and they knew I needed help if there was any chance of getting past this.

Chapter 3

Trip to New York from Hell

The last week of that December my family and I were set to leave on a trip to New York City. For my sister and me, this was our first time in the Big Apple, and we were excited because it was the best time of year to go: Christmas.

I actually still remember the night before when we packed our bags. I was excited about my new pink polka dot bag that I was going to bring on the plane with me, and I busied myself with cramming everything I thought I might need into it. In between stuffing packs of gum and tissues into my bag, I remember feeling weird that night but having no idea that I was having anxiety about traveling. It was a whole new feeling, and my brain really didn't know how to handle it– at the time I didn't even know what anxiety was.

The next morning, everything seemed okay; we got through the airport and made it onto our flight without a problem. And when we touched down in New York, there was nothing but excitement about the coming week. But it didn't last very long. Because when we got to the hotel, all hell broke loose.

My parents went to go check us in while my sister and I waited in the chairs in the lobby. And for some reason, I just started bawling. Not controlled tears though– it was full-on ugly crying. I sat there not really knowing why I was so upset, and I certainly couldn't think of a way to make myself stop. So I just cried. On the floor. In the crowded lobby of a huge hotel.

You can imagine how my parents felt coming back from the reception desk to see their kid distraught and in tears on the floor with people staring at her. They immediately asked if I was okay while simultaneously looking for signs of anything being wrong. That was the problem– there was nothing wrong. I was totally fine, and I couldn't give them an explanation for my sudden breakdown.

So we hurried up to our room, me still crying, my parents thoroughly freaked out, and my sister looking at me like I had just sprouted a new arm. In the room, I begged my mom to take my temperature, because I thought that had to be what was making me feel so bad; I had to be sick. That was the only logical explanation.

When she told me it was one degree higher than normal body temperature, I went into something I would consider quite close to full blown hysterics. I begged my mom to give me medicine, thinking that would make me feel better– anything to stop feeling like *this*.

(It took me years to finally be able to identify what I was feeling that night. That overwhelming sense of dread that something was going to go wrong and the restlessness? That was anxiety.)

I really don't know how we made it through the rest of that night with the way I was carrying on, but the placebo effect of that medicine must have kicked in, because somehow we all made it to the next morning.

After waking up and getting dressed, we decided to walk down to get breakfast at a little grocery place, looking forward to a busy day of sight-seeing ahead of us. I had calmed down to a certain extent, but I was still really uneasy, and going to the store didn't change that.

When we got there, it didn't take long for my parents to realize that there was a new development in my ever-growing list of alarming symptoms: I refused to eat anything. My parents were, to say the least, shocked. Usually, I would have never passed up the opportunity to eat the pastries in the bakery section for breakfast, but that morning I wasn't feeling it. My parents eventually convinced me to eat something, at least so I wouldn't get hungry until lunch, and I agreed to eat a doughnut. But even after sitting down at a table, I still hesitated to eat, sitting there absently until my parents reminded me to take bites of my breakfast.

We ate at that grocery place every morning for breakfast for the rest of the trip. And for the rest of the trip I refused to eat anything other than a doughnut from that specific bakery for breakfast.

After breakfast, we were off to all of the popular tourist attractions, but it was obvious I wasn't feeling like myself. I struggled through the sightseeing at the Statue of Liberty, was visibly upset for no reason at the American Girl Doll Store, and barely made it through all of the museums.

My behavior had changed so drastically and was so unpredictable, in fact, that my parents thought I had developed a pretty serious blood sugar condition like diabetes that would affect my mood and how I acted if my sugar got too low. They tried to make sure that I always had some kind of sugar in my system, just in case, so that we could at least make it through the week and go home for me to get checked out by a doctor. But that was close to impossible when I flat out refused to eat anything.

That night, my mom walked down to the shop around the corner from our hotel and bought peanut butter crackers and sugar tablets that diabetics use to elevate their blood sugar, with the hopes that they would help the next time I got upset. Ideally, by raising my glucose levels, I wouldn't have such unpredictable mood swings.

The next day we put it to the test, my parents making me eat a snack whenever my mood seemed to go downhill. And by that evening we had our conclusion: it didn't work. Even with the snacks, I still inexplicably got upset and shut down several times throughout the day. My parents were at a loss.

For the rest of the trip, I refused to eat more and more frequently, much to my parents' dismay. I didn't want to do anything or go anywhere, and I had become quite emotionally unstable despite my family's efforts to figure out what the problem was and make me comfortable. Nothing helped, and as much as I tried, I couldn't pinpoint what was making me feel that way. How are you supposed to tell someone what's wrong when you don't even know what the problem is?

Chapter 4

Finding a Little Clarity

As soon as we got back to New Orleans my parents started a massive hunt for a doctor that would explain what was wrong with me. I saw several doctors who dismissed my "affliction" as an eating disorder and said that I should see a therapist; but none of them could definitively diagnose me. My parents continued their search, certain that my behavior could not be explained by the symptoms of an eating disorder.

In the meantime, I began to stop eating altogether. When my mom and dad offered me a food such as cheese, I would refuse, saying that I had already eaten some the day before. When they offered foods like Pop Tarts I would decline because it "had too much sugar." I also turned down any foods that had eggs or meat in them or that had any potential of having come into contact with eggs or meat.

My food intake was extremely limited, even though my parents begged me to eat every single day, their ultimate fear being that I would starve myself to death. I lost weight at a dangerously rapid pace and showed no signs of beginning to eat again any time soon. This only seemed to strengthen the doctors' conclusions that I had an eating disorder. I was quickly referred to a nutritionist and a therapist that specialized in eating disorders, and I began seeing them both on a weekly basis. But nothing seemed to be helping, and I simply continued on my downward spiral caused by something we couldn't identify.

While we were still searching for answers to that issue, another one arose that was just as weird– I started obsessively washing my hands. You wouldn't really think that would be a bad obsession, right? But it was. I washed my hands before breakfast in the morning, after breakfast, before brushing my teeth, after brushing my teeth, before lunch, after lunch, before dinner, after dinner, before brushing my teeth at night, and after brushing my teeth. That's ten times a day not including my handwashing after using the bathroom throughout the day and after touching things that were "contaminated". Sometimes, I would just get the urge to wash my hands for no reason– and I would.

The amount of times I washed my hands a day wasn't even really the biggest problem. The issue was that every single time I washed my hands I would wash them for *at least* two full minutes. I remember standing by the sink and scrubbing my hands while singing the "Happy Birthday" song, because I had seen somewhere that you should wash your hands for the duration of the song in order for them to be fully clean.

I would sing the song in my head, sing it again, get more soap, sing the song again, then again, and repeat that process for as long as I felt it was necessary. The process could range from two minutes to upwards of five minutes, at which time my parents had to intervene and make me stop. It quickly got to the point where I cleaned my hands so many times a day that I would actually end up washing off the first few layers of my skin. My hands were raw, cracked, and bleeding even though my parents constantly kept lotion on them. Things began to look pretty grim, and my weird behavior seemed to get worse with each day that passed.

My parents' horror only grew when one of the nurses told my mom that I was exhibiting classic after-effects of being sexually abused. They asked her if I had gone anywhere alone recently or if I had slept over at a friend's house. Fearing the worst, my mom raked her memory for any time this could have happened but came up empty every time.

Looking back, she felt helpless, having to give everyone in our lives a second look, even people we had known for years. She knew there was no way sexual abuse was even a possibility, but with the doctors unable to account for my strange behavior, she had to take everything into account. She began questioning if she could trust everyone I came into contact with at school or on weekends, but eventually came to the conclusion that she had known to be true the whole time– something else was wrong.

When that possibility was exhausted, the doctors began questioning if my behavior was due to drugs. Once again, they asked my mom if I had been out of her sight recently or exposed to drugs in any way. And once again, she had to take a look at everyone we knew, even though she was sure no one in my life would have given me access to drugs. Obviously, after investigating every little possibility, my mom came to the same conclusion she had about the sexual abuse, and she only became more determined than ever to find someone who knew what was actually wrong with me.

Then we found a doctor named Dr. Anderson, and not only did he know what was really wrong with me, but he also knew what to do about it. All of my symptoms and weird behaviors pointed towards PANDAS, or Pediatric Autoimmune Neuropsychiatric Disorder Associated with Streptococcal Infections. PANDAS results from streptococcus bacteria invading and multiplying in the brain. In response, the immune system then sends antibodies to destroy the bacteria, but they also end up attacking the brain in the process. PANDAS comes with a whole slew of symptoms, one of which is OCD; I also had other manifestations, including the development of a tic, bouts of anxiety, changes in academic ability, and frequent mood swings.

The only problem and reason none of the previous doctors would diagnose me with PANDAS was because I had never actually gotten a strep diagnosis, which previously had been a necessary requirement for a PANDAS diagnosis. Even though I had gotten sick in December, there was never any proof that strep was the cause. And because PANDAS is associated with streptococcus infections, none of the other doctors diagnosed me with it.

What made Dr. Anderson able to give me a definitive diagnosis was the new evidence that PANDAS isn't always associated with strep. More and more research was emerging showing that not all cases of the disorder have that origin. Therefore, even though I had never actually had strep, it was still possible that the problems I was having came as a result of PANDAS. In fact, all of my recent behaviors seemed to indicate that that was indeed the cause.

With a diagnosis finally out of the way, the next step was treatment. By this point, I had already lost around fifteen pounds from refusing to eat, and my list of unhealthy behaviors grew on a daily basis. Recognizing the urgency of the situation, my pediatrician admitted me to the hospital where they pumped me with IGG, which would fight against what was going on inside of my brain.

I remember the day I was admitted. It was a school day, and I woke up way later than usual; I ran downstairs to see what was going on, expecting inclement weather to be what was keeping me home. Instead, my mom lifted me onto her lap and calmly explained that I wasn't going to school that day because I was actually going to the hospital. The next thing I knew I was in the car.

Looking back now, I realize that I had no idea at the time what was happening. I didn't really know what went on at hospitals besides people going there when they were really sick or hurt, and in my mind, I didn't fit into either of those categories. I was completely oblivious to the fact that something was seriously wrong with me and that my situation was really urgent.

The first memory I have of being in the hospital is when I got my IV. Both my parents were with me, and I was blissfully unaware that the nurse was about to stick a huge needle into my hand. They made me sit back and look away so I wouldn't see what they were doing while my parents sang a nursery song to distract me, which was, apparently, all it took for me to get distracted. When the nurse was done, I picked out a sticker, and that was that.

Or so I thought. Not too long after getting the IV, though, I became extremely conscious of the needle in my hand. When I looked at it there was some blood backing up into the tubing, and I got pretty upset at the sight of it. To be honest, I don't know how my parents dealt with me after that, because I cried almost nonstop for the rest of that two-day, one-night stay in the pediatric unit. Even though I was trying my best to be brave, I was doing a pretty horrible job of staying calm.

I don't remember a lot after that, but the snippets that I do remember are either really good or really bad. I do remember that the Girl Scouts in my troop wrote me letters and brought me a hot pink, heart-shaped pillow to try to cheer me up, a family friend stopped by to give me some encouragement, and my uncle and cousins visited bearing the gift of a stuffed lion. One of the nurses even brought me a popsicle, and in hindsight, I'm sure that if I hadn't been so scared that we could have had a pretty decent party.

My next memory is of me refusing to eat a Lunchable that my dad tried to feed me because I wasn't "allowed" to eat it. My parents tried to comfort me by assuring me that they gave me full permission to eat it, but I made it very clear that that was not what I meant. Something in my brain was telling me that I couldn't do it, and no amount of outside encouragement would yield a different result.

That night was one of the longest nights of my life (and probably of my mom's life too). I was on the right side of the hospital bed while she was on the left, because I couldn't seem to calm down enough to sleep without her next to me. Even when she was next to me, we barely got any sleep; I kept repeating "No I'm not. I don't even know why I said that," out loud over and over and over. I had recently started doing this at home, and no one was very fond of it– especially my sister, with whom I insisted I share a room, and my mom, who had to sleep with me on a blow-up mattress on my sister's floor every night. I think everyone was hoping that this practice wouldn't continue at the hospital, but instead it seemed to have intensified. No one knew why I was doing it, and I couldn't explain it, so that's how we spent that night (and many nights before that) until I finally dozed off.

The next day, I woke up feeling upset and frustrated that I couldn't go home. So, at a point in the day when I was feeling particularly anxious, my mom took me down to the pediatric unit's playroom, and we used dot markers to make pictures. My mom made up a story about a king, a queen, and a chicken to get my mind off things, but it only distracted me for a short amount of time. Despite her best efforts, I just kept getting more and more upset, and eventually we decided to go back to my room. (Evidently, I must have looked way more miserable than I thought I did on the way out, because a nurse stopped me and let me pick out a toy to take back to the room.)

That evening, when I was about to be discharged, I got an awful migraine, which is a common side effect of the treatment I was receiving. The headache just made my already miserable hospital stay even more interesting. On a scale of 1 to 10 the pain was a 12, but there wasn't really anything we could do about it. My mom resorted to filling unused latex gloves with ice and positioning them around my head in a frozen glove-halo hoping that this would help with the pain. Unfortunately, they didn't do much.

And much to my horror, the time finally came when I had to get my IV taken out. Obviously, this doesn't really seem like a big deal, but to six-year-old me it was the equivalent of the apocalypse.

If the headache didn't already have me in tears, the thought of someone taking my IV out certainly did. By the time the nurses were actually ready to take it out, I had already worked myself into hysteria.

I must have looked like a complete mess– a crying six-year-old lying in a pile of ice-filled latex gloves while frantically trying to keep away from the nurse. But somehow, they managed to get to my hand, and I closed my eyes, bracing myself for the worst pain of my life as they took the IV out. The nurse didn't do anything for a few seconds, so I opened my eyes to see what was taking them so long, and it turned out that they had, in fact, already taken it out.

I don't remember anything from that night after that. I don't remember leaving the hospital or the drive home or making my way upstairs to my room and getting into my own bed for the first time in months, instead of the air mattress on my sister's floor. I don't even remember if I did my repetitions of "No I'm not. I don't even know why I said that." I just hoped that when I woke up things would be better.

Chapter 5

Now What?

After my brief stint in the hospital for medical treatment, it was finally time for my psychological treatment. I started to see a therapist that specialized in eating disorders, Mrs. H, with the hopes that my behavior would return to normal pretty quickly (wishful thinking).

While we worked, we came to refer to my OCD and anxiety as "PANDAS Brain," which made it much easier for me to talk about. Instead of trying to explain that my brain was somehow telling me that I couldn't do certain things, I could say that my PANDAS Brain didn't allow it. It took on its own identity, playing the villain in my brain that wouldn't shut up. Sometimes I would try to talk to it and tell it how unreasonable it was being. Once, I wrote a letter to it, and Mrs. H gave me permission to use all the bad words I wanted. The point was, by giving my anxiety and OCD a name, it was much easier for me to identify that part of me as foreign, and hopefully I wouldn't feel like I was arguing with myself. It helped me see that my PANDAS Brain was the problem– not me.

I referred to my anxiety and OCD as "PANDAS Brain" for years after that. Not only was it more convenient, but it also personified the part of me that I was battling every day. It was no longer just a "feeling" that something was telling me I couldn't do something. Now it was an actual thing, capable of telling me whatever it wanted. "PANDAS Brain" seemed to cover every base without me ever having to actually say OCD and anxiety. So that was the term that served as the basis of every therapy session, and that came to be the name for the tyrannical voice in my head.

During my sessions with Mrs. H, I managed to figure out some of my previous and recurring rituals in order to try to control them better in the future. We eventually found that all of the rituals I had spent so much time on came back to theoretically preventing one seemingly petty thing: vomiting.

Obviously, no one likes to vomit, but we found that that was the fear my OCD had zeroed in on. I obsessed over it. Specifically, I obsessed over trying to prevent it from happening to me by any means necessary. This explained everything– why I stopped eating, why I washed my hands for minutes at a time, why I had trouble doing normal, everyday things. Every single thing that I did brought an immense amount of anxiety that I had to get through using rituals and rules that I set for myself.

All of my fears were directly correlated to the weird things that I had started doing before my diagnosis. For example, I stopped eating anything that contained meat, because I was afraid that I would come into contact with raw or undercooked meat and get food poisoning, which would lead to vomiting. I couldn't even touch meat, because if I contaminated my hands with it I would have to start my hand washing ritual, which was painful and annoying, even for me.

I stopped eating anything with egg in it for pretty much the same reason. I thought that if I came into contact with raw egg I could end up getting sick, and I was not about to take that chance. So I cut it out of my diet. I couldn't touch them either; the fact that they had shells made no difference in my mind.

This really limited my diet and played a big role in my rapid weight loss. I refused to eat anything that even had the smallest chance of coming into contact with eggs or meat, and I looked at the ingredients on boxes of food to make sure it was safe before eating. If it was even processed in the same facility as something with meat or egg in it, it was off limits.

I also cut out foods that I thought contained a lot of sugar because of a bad experience I had had as a kid. (My mom, sister, cousin, and aunt went on a little trip to a hotel and, throughout the day, us kids consumed an insane amount of candy. That night, my sister and I got extremely sick, and we ended up all going home.) I had taken that memory of getting sick and associated it with the amount of candy that I had eaten that day. I felt that the amount of sugar that I consumed was the reason I vomited, and therefore tried to cut sugar from my diet to the best of my ability.

This obviously shouldn't have been a huge problem. I would read the nutritional facts on the back of the food boxes and try to find something with the least amount of sugar, which was harmless enough. But my PANDAS Brain took it to the extreme. Everything had at least a little sugar, and I thought that any sugar at all was too much. So my answer to that was to simply not eat at all. That's why I refused to eat Pop Tarts (my usual breakfast) and just about any food with more than five grams of sugar. My parents had to either break my arm to get me to eat or find a way to make sure I didn't get a look at how much sugar was in my food.

Another rule that stemmed from that experience in the hotel was that I was not allowed to eat Chinese food. It seems like the simplest thing, but I couldn't do it. Looking back to the night we had stayed in the hotel, we had ordered Chinese food for dinner, and something in my head told me that it was one of the reasons I had gotten sick that night. So, no more. Ever.

I even made a rule from a specific experience that I had earlier in second grade. Every morning before school, I would eat the same breakfast because it was fast and easy. One particular day, though, I started to feel a little weird right before lunch time. I started having a lot of anxiety and felt what I thought was the beginning of vomiting. I never actually vomited, but I went home from school feeling exceptionally freaked out.

I couldn't figure out what had really happened that day, but I thought it was only logical to stop doing the only thing that I thought may have been the cause: repetitive eating habits. I reasoned that I had gotten sick because I had eaten the same thing that morning as I had the morning before and the morning before. So from then on, if I ate a certain food one day, I was not allowed to eat it the next day. My brain convinced me that it would still be in my stomach, which would lead to me getting sick, just like it had on that day at school.

And God forbid I ate the same thing twice in one day! That would have been even worse than eating the same thing two days in a row. I was very vigilant in remembering what I was and wasn't allowed to eat depending on the amount of time it had been since the last time I had eaten it. I felt like there was no other way; I had to keep myself safe.

One of the more specific restrictions that I had was that I could not eat vanilla pudding or pretzels, because I got sick one night after I had eaten those snacks at school for snack-time. In my mind the only logical explanation for me getting sick was that I had eaten those two foods together earlier in the day. So no more pretzels or vanilla pudding.

One of the most memorable rules I had was that I had to eat things throughout the day that could go together well to form a cohesive meal. I couldn't eat anything that would possibly "not mix well" in my stomach with something I had eaten earlier, because, again, I thought that the food I ate during the day would be there all day. So it was only logical that if I didn't eat foods that would complement each other I would get sick.

For example, if I ate a banana for breakfast, I couldn't have a hamburger for lunch because those two things don't typically go together. If I had a banana for breakfast, I would have to have something like yogurt for lunch, because those things traditionally go well together.

Obviously, these rules restricted my food choices immensely, and most of the time, I felt it was easier to just not eat. And those are just a few of the rules I had to follow. That list doesn't even include the rules for why I washed my hands until they were raw or why I couldn't function in my daily life. There were totally different sets of rules and rituals for that.

Some of the rituals and anxiety did actually stem from twisted logic, but there were also rules that were more superstitious in nature. Instead of the situation being "doing this could lead to getting contaminated somehow, which could lead to me getting sick" it was "if I do this or don't do this I will get sick". And that threat involved everything. I couldn't walk through the house without my brain trying to tell me to use a specific hallway or else get sick. Then, when I started walking down that corridor, I would just get the threat that I would actually get sick if I used that hallway. That's why I couldn't pick which hallway to use when my mom found me crying by the stairs. I couldn't make decisions on the most trivial things for fear that the wrong choice would result in me getting sick.

I made *tons* of stupid rules in an attempt to "protect" myself. There were just as many at home as there were at school, and some of my coping mechanisms kept me from doing regular activities there. Just the thought of going to P.E. class during the school day left me so panicked that I couldn't do anything except cry. Instead, every time that class met, I would go and talk to the counselor who helped me manage my anxiety while the poor P.E. teacher did her best to figure out what to do with me.

Eventually, I was able to figure out my reasoning behind avoiding P.E.– it was the exact same one that restricted me from doing so many other things. I was scared that it would make me sick.

You're probably wondering how a second grade P.E. class could possibly make you sick. Picture this: the entire second grade class running around on a blacktop in the heat of a New Orleans day. Students got overheated and overexerted themselves pretty often, and I had seen my fair share of kids throwing up after P.E. or recess. In my mind, getting overheated or being too active resulted in vomiting, so obviously I felt the need to stay inside with the counselor so that I wouldn't be at risk. It was a real stretch, but my PANDAS Brain made it sound perfectly logical.

Because I attended a Catholic school, the entire student body would walk over to Church every Wednesday. (Yes, every Wednesday.) And, as luck would have it, that was another place I couldn't go. Maybe it was the fact that sitting in Mass left me alone with my thoughts for an hour, and I ended up getting a panic attack, or maybe it was the fact that while my class was rehearsing for First Communion my friend next to me vomited inside the church, and it was now contaminated. Maybe it was the fact that the Church had horrible ventilation, and this often led to students getting sick (vomiting) during the Mass. Maybe it was a combination of all three, but whether it was a school Mass or a Mass on Sunday, I *could not* do it.

If I tried to get through a Mass, I had a panic attack before, during, or after the service without fail. It didn't even matter which church I was in. I didn't have to be in the one where we went for school Masses; I could be at the one close to my house, and for some reason it had the same effect on me. Any Mass at any church anywhere in New Orleans or elsewhere would end the same way: either in tears or with a panic attack.

The school counselor, Mrs. Lisa, whom I had become great friends with after spending every P.E. class in her office, tried everything to get me through a Mass. She gave me a little finger puppet to distract me enough to avoid a panic attack, she went to Church with me, she even convinced me to join the choir, because that would keep my mind busy.

But nothing worked. The finger puppet couldn't take my mind off my fears of getting sick, and the choir attempt ended in me having a full-fledge panic attack halfway through the Mass. I ended up sobbing while I ran to where Mrs. Lisa sat, which was probably mildly terrifying for all the other Church-goers.

We tried for years to figure out any way for me to make it through a Mass. I mean, they happened every Wednesday and then again when my family went on Sunday. Unfortunately, despite everyone's best efforts, I ended up not being able to sit through an entire Mass without having an anxiety attack until seventh grade.

Chapter 6

My School-Savior, Mrs. Lisa

Before second grade, I didn't know what Mrs. Lisa did at my school. In fact, I didn't even know who she was. The first time we met, she introduced herself as the school counselor while we stood by the stairs, and I didn't think anything would come from it. I didn't even know what a counselor was.

But after that, we scheduled regular meetings up in her office, where we worked and talked through what was making me anxious, playing games as we did. When I was there, I never felt like we were actually doing any work, but Mrs. Lisa found a way to get me to open up to her about what was worrying me through games and pictures and toys. Sometimes we put on puppet shows, and sometimes we played board games; but no matter what we did, it was always fun.

That might have had something to do with Mrs. Lisa's office itself. She had a dream office tucked up inside a quiet stairwell in the middle of the school. I never knew what that room was before we met, and after seeing what was inside I was disappointed that I didn't know about it earlier. It was a small room, maybe one third the size of all the other classrooms, separated into two sections: Mrs. Lisa's office, with her desk and computer, and the play area, with an amazing array of games and toys.

She had a fish tank with a few small fish in it that I could feed when I visited her. She had a kitchen drawer sized sandbox and a pig-shaped brush to go with it; she had a dry erase board with the best markers I had ever seen to write on it with. She had a shelf full of action figures, a basket of toy soldiers, a bucket of doll house components, and even a fake doctor kit. I have vivid memories from several occasions when I pretended that she was my patient in the hospital and authenticated the experience with a red marker dot on her hand in the exact same place I had had my IV. Needless to say, this office was *the* place to be when I was having anxiety; I always felt safest when I was there. It was my sanctuary.

Mrs. Lisa and I also just talked a lot there, and I never felt like she was judging me or trying to play the role of a therapist. I genuinely saw her as a friend who cared about me, and in truth, I think I opened up more to her than I did with my actual therapist. I looked forward to meeting with her at least once every week and sent her notes on days we didn't get a chance to see each other. Her note-receiving system was so perfect that I even wrote to her on days when we did meet. (She had a little wooden box set up in the main office with a locking lid and a slot that was perfect for dropping letters in, along with a flowerpot full of slips of paper and pens for us to use.)

Unfortunately, even the activity I loved so much, writing her notes, couldn't go without a compulsion. Any time I wrote about how my day or week was going I had to end the sentence with "so far" so that I wouldn't jinx myself. So, if I wanted to say that I was having a good day, I would have written "I'm having a good day so far," because I feared that my day would end up going bad. And the ultimate bad day for me involved vomiting.

Sometimes, I just drew her pictures, and she made sure to tell me that she appreciated each and every one.

And every Wednesday I went to the main office of the school while everyone else walked over to church, and together we went up to her office that soon became a second home. On days when Mrs. Lisa wasn't there when it was time for Mass, I would either have a panic attack while the people in the main office tried to usher me off to church or make up an excuse to call my mom so I could hear her voice (this option usually resulted in uncontrollable crying).

On days when there wasn't Mass, I still saw Mrs. Lisa. I saw her whenever I was feeling stressed or anxious, and after every appointment I left her office feeling lighter than I had when I walked in. Even when we didn't have an appointment scheduled I would pull her aside every now and then during the day if I needed her, and we could escape to her office.

She always knew how to calm my anxiety and talk me out of my panic. If there was ever a day when she wasn't at school when I needed her, my panic would intensify, and I would usually end up going home, because I couldn't function academically as a result. Just knowing that she was in the school building was comforting to me, and on the rare days when she wasn't there, the school felt empty.

As much as I tried to not depend on her as a crutch, I found it almost impossible to make it through the day without her help. I felt like my entire world was turned upside down, and she was the constant I had to keep me stable while I was at school. It was almost like she made me feel like I had some control in an environment where I didn't have a lot of power over what happened. Her being in my corner made me feel like maybe my school situation wasn't absolutely hopeless.

To sum it all up, Mrs. Lisa was one of my best guardian angels. She helped me start to get my life back when I didn't even know that it had been taken from me in the first place, and I'll be grateful for that for the rest of my life.

Chapter 7

Therapy: Never a Friend to Me

I'm not going to lie; a lot of my early therapy sessions are a blur; the only ones I really remember are the ones that I found most traumatizing. I remember a lot of my therapist's and my techniques to get the obsessions to stop, though, despite the fact that they all ended up failing in one way or another.

One of the first things Mrs. H and I did together was meant to lessen my "sticky thoughts," which is what we called my obsessive thoughts. She gave me a little blue portfolio with sticky notes and a pen inside. The idea was that whenever I would get a troubling thought that wouldn't go away, I would write it down on the sticky note and stick it to my head. I would then symbolically transfer that thought to the sticky note, then take it off my head and put it in the portfolio. This was the first tool we ever tried to use to calm me down when my thoughts were getting particularly overwhelming. Needless to say, it didn't work in any way, shape, or form.

I remember one specific night when I was feeling particularly anxious, and I started to feel a little sick as a result (my early panic attacks manifested as nausea, which then worsened the panic), setting off all sorts of alarms in my brain that then increased my anxiety. I ran downstairs, grabbed my portfolio, and desperately tried to transfer the thought to the sticky note so I would be free from that horrible feeling. My mom was washing dishes a few feet away, so I tried to be subtle– if I told her I was feeling sick then it would be too real. So instead I stood there frantically putting a sticky note on my head, taking it off, putting it back on, taking it off…

It didn't work. Within seconds I was in full panic mode, and I told my mom that I was not feeling well in what probably turned out to be just one long word instead of an actual sentence. We rushed into her bathroom where I sat on the floor waiting for something to happen.

I felt terrible, and my mind was going faster than the speed of light. After about half an hour with no change I actually remember looking over at my mom and telling her that I wanted to die. If from then on my life was just going to be constant anxiety that had the power to make me feel so sick and that made me too scared to go about regular activities as simple as eating, I told her that I didn't see the point in living. I was eight. And that was the first panic attack I have full recollection of.

During one of my actual therapy sessions, Mrs. H and I had a little lunch date in her office so that she could try to convince me to eat. She told me to get my favorite thing from McDonald's (a cheeseburger Happy Meal), which I wasn't allowed to eat given the restrictions my OCD had constructed and bring it in so that we could eat together.

Even before my diagnosis, I had stopped eating meat, because, no matter what kind it was, I thought it had to be all the way cooked or else I would get food poisoning. Food poisoning in my brain equaled vomiting. Even things that could safely be cooked rare like steak or burgers had to be cooked all the way through. Instead of dealing with the anxiety that came with wondering if my meat was cooked, I had just cut it out of my diet completely.

After my parents pleaded with me every day to eat something other than yogurt (I pretty much lived off yogurt, because it was one of the few foods that fit within my restrictions) for months, I finally came up with a way that would make it possible. I still didn't eat meat very much at all, but at least I could when my parents felt like I needed to eat something other than yogurt.

My plan was, I would cut all of my meat as usual, but before putting every bite in my mouth I would ask my parents if it was cooked all the way. I felt like if my parents told me that it was cooked, then there was no way they could possibly be wrong, therefore eliminating the risk of food poisoning. I have vivid memories of my parents feeding me my dinner, and between every bite, I had to ask if what I had on my fork was cooked. I only allowed them to put the food in my mouth after they confirmed that the food was indeed cooked.

So even though I don't really have any specific memories of that lunch date/therapy appointment with Mrs. H, I'm one hundred percent sure it just involved me asking her "Is this cooked?" before every bite. Obviously, the session didn't have any effect on my meat ritual, because it continued for a long time. After months, I was able to shorten it to asking once if my food was cooked before I ate anything. Even after years of therapy and the eventual end of that particular ritual, I still relapse every now and then, asking my parents if my food is cooked before eating it, just to be sure.

We tried a lot of weird things in therapy, anything that had the possibility of helping me overcome my fear. One day, my therapy session involved me finger-painting with pudding in an attempt to lessen my fear of it from that incident in kindergarten involving the vanilla pudding. It sounds stupid, but the idea behind it was that I would come into contact with the pudding as much as possible by having it all over my hands but not actually eating it (I had made it very clear that that was not an option). We used chocolate pudding instead of vanilla pudding too, because I couldn't even think of using vanilla pudding– that would have been way too much to handle.

Simply thinking about touching vanilla pudding left me in a panic, and the goal of the activity was to lessen my anxiety, not to send me into a full-blown panic attack. While using a different flavor of pudding brought down my anxiety level a little bit, it didn't eliminate it by any means, and it turned out to be a tough exercise for me. After that, I allowed myself to eat chocolate pudding for a very brief amount of time, but that ended fairly quickly after I decided I had pushed my luck for too long already. To this day, I have not come into contact with vanilla pudding, and I hope to keep it that way.

Later on in my relationship with Mrs. H, she decided that our next goal would be for me to put on a robe that I had not been able to wear since I had vomited while wearing it a few years before. I hadn't even been able to touch it since then, even though my mom had thoroughly washed it. This session was particularly terrible for me, so I remember it pretty clearly.

My mom packed up the robe in a plastic grocery bag since I refused to touch it, and we went to see Mrs. H. When we got there, she started the exposure by having me touch the robe, and I hadn't anticipated how difficult it would be. In my mind, that robe had all the germs in it that went with throw up. So obviously if I put it on or even touched it those germs would get on me, and I would end up getting sick by the end of the night. See my OCD logic?

Just touching it ramped up my anxiety tremendously, but we weren't done. Next, she made me actually put the robe on, and I completely lost it. I stood there in her office with one arm in a blue leopard print robe and sobbed. There was absolutely no doubt in my mind now that I would get sick. And I was hysterical. I had spent so much time following rules that I set to protect myself from getting sick, and it only took seconds for that to be wasted by ensuring that I would throw up when I put on the robe.

I was horrified about what was going to happen. I was horrified about what I had let happen; I had just allowed myself to be contaminated. By the time we left the appointment, I was still in a panic, and I waited for the inevitable sickness that would ensue. Later that night, when nothing happened, I praised the heavens that I had gotten lucky and promised myself that I would never let myself be so stupid again.

That's pretty much how the rest of second grade year and the majority of third grade year went– exposure after exposure. Most of the time they just amplified my anxiety instead of reducing it, and I started having panic attacks in the evenings after almost every therapy session.

On top of all of that, my psychiatrist was trying to figure out the correct medication dosages and combinations. He put me on one medicine for a few months, saw no change, weened me off of it, and prescribed a new one. When the new one didn't work the process would start over. My family and I were always one the lookout for the side effects of each prescription, which ranged from increase in appetite to uncontrollable body tremors. Over a span of a few months, we plowed through at least four different medications, none of which seemed to be working the way we needed them to.

The only medication that had any beneficial effect on me whatsoever was fluoxetine, and even that didn't stop all of the symptoms or bring down my anxiety levels as much as it was supposed to– it just made them bearable.

But I still had a lot of hope that my OCD would lose its prevalence, and as long as my family was there to support me, I agreed to dive headfirst into therapy in an attempt to get my life back.

Chapter 8

The Art of Distraction

My third-grade year was kind of uneventful compared to previous ones, except for the fact that right before the school year started my mom had my twin brothers two months prematurely. They stayed in the hospital for a long time, and when they finally came home my parents knew they needed help to take care of them during the night. They hired a really nice lady named Winnie to help so that they could at least get a little sleep (in theory).

This is one of the periods of my life from which I have very little memory, but I still remember waking up early almost every morning before school and walking over to the boys' room when my anxiety level would inevitably elevate after having too much time alone with my thoughts.

I would walk in as quietly as possible and always find my mom and Winnie trying one method or another to get my brothers to go back to sleep. I felt comforted simply by being in the same room as them, and after the first few mornings I did this, it almost started to become a daily routine.

My mom even told me that she had heard Winnie talking to one of the twins, telling him that I would probably be showing up soon and taking up residence on the floor just like I had every morning before that. That's just kind of how it was. Before the sun was out, I would sneak into their room and stay there until it was time to get ready for school, because that was all I needed to get that bit of anxiety to go away.

I tried to help with my brothers as much as possible, and I took every opportunity I could to change their diapers or feed them. After being the youngest child for so long, I took my job as a big sister very seriously, and I found that if nothing else, taking care of them was a good distraction. It never failed to take my mind off my worries, even if only for a little while, and I was willing to take all the relief I could get.

I think this was also about the time that I started realizing that my anxiety got much worse when I was free with my thoughts. I started dreading going to places like assemblies or even to bed because I knew that there was nothing to distract me there, nothing to focus on except my brain pointing out all the possible ways I could come into contact with germs and get sick. For me it was torture, so I tried my best to never be caught in a situation where I didn't have something that could distract me, be it rereading a pamphlet I had already read 5,000 times before or counting ceiling tiles one by one.

By the time fourth grade rolled around, one of the only things that we really knew for certain was that structure helped ease my anxiety. Other than that, we couldn't really pinpoint what heightened or lessened my worry. But after being pretty disappointed that I got a new fourth grade teacher named Ms. C instead of Mrs. Garry (the nicest teacher ever), I was hopeful that I would find a way to make it work.

Not long into the year, Ms. C started missing weeks of school at a time. The rest of my classmates and I had a daily rotation of substitute teachers who tried their best but couldn't run the class sufficiently given the fact that they were kind of just thrown into the middle of things with barely any preparation. The class became fairly chaotic and lost most, if not all, of its structure.

This obviously didn't mesh well with my pre-existing anxiety and OCD symptoms, as it caused me to become more anxious, which meant an increase in compulsive rituals. Dr. H suggested that I transfer to a different class to avoid any unnecessary anxiety, and I was moved into none other than Mrs. Garry's classroom. It was amazing, and I quickly found out that I had no time to be upset about leaving my friends from Ms. C's class, because, after about a month without a permanent teacher, the rest of Ms. C's class was divided into the two other classrooms (one belonging to Mrs. Garry and the other belonging to another teacher).

That was a pretty exciting (and chaotic) school year, and looking back, I'm kind of surprised that I got through it so easily. I attribute most of my success to my weekly meetings with Mrs. Lisa, which allowed me to de-stress while I was still at school and talk about how lots of the things that I was panicking about were completely irrational.

As I got into the swing of fourth grade, my brothers were around a year old, and I still thought they were pretty cute for the most part. But there was one problem. Because they were born so prematurely, one of my brothers had some kind of flap in his throat that wasn't supposed to be there. And it wasn't really too big of an issue in his day-to-day functioning… until it was feeding time.

We would feed this child, and he would proceed to cough until he projectile vomited the contents of his stomach all over the kitchen. At least once a week. It was genuinely just like the stuff I had nightmares about, but this was real, and it sent me into a panic attack every time.

I tried to be rational with myself. I knew he wasn't actually sick, so there was no way I could catch germs from him. I knew that it technically wasn't even vomit, since he had literally just eaten then thrown it all back up. But it didn't matter one bit. Every single time my brother started coughing after eating, my heart would speed all the way up, and I would get ready to move. When the inevitable would indeed happen, I would sprint away from the dinner table and lock myself in my room for the next few days to escape the germs, only leaving for school and going back in as soon as I got home.

I tried my best to stay involved with my brothers, even though the whole projectile vomiting thing definitely made it harder. I remained optimistic that we would all be able to get past this. Eventually, my brother's throat flap thing would go away, and hopefully, my anxiety would get better. Until then, I did what I could, and I counted every day my brother didn't vomit as a blessing.

I also continued to see Dr. H once a week to work on understanding that what my PANDAS Brain told me I wasn't allowed to do actually had no connection to vomiting. One session, she and I sat on the floor and listed all of the different types of ways someone could say "vomit," which at this time I called T.U. (short for throw up) because I was not even allowed to say the words or else it would happen.

I remember that session being especially anxiety-inducing, because I wasn't even allowed to say "throw up," and I was tasked with coming up with other ways of conveying the same idea. That day I learned some new euphemisms that I hadn't known before, and honestly, I probably could have lived a happy life without knowing that "tossing your cookies" means vomiting, but I like to think it helped a little in the long run.

Chapter 9

Grades 5-7: Silence is Not Golden

Fifth grade is when you're actually looked at as big kids by the other students (or so we thought), and it was fantastic. Well… it started fantastic. I was comfortable with the classmates I had grown up with, and I felt ready for whatever came my way. All I had to do was make sure my anxiety didn't get the best of me. And I hoped that wouldn't be too hard with the help of my appointments with Mrs. Lisa and Mrs. H.

But not long into my fifth-grade year, my PANDAS Brain came up with the best idea it had ever had: I would stop talking in the school building. There was absolutely no way I could mess this up. All I had to do was keep my mouth shut. The goal was, by not opening my mouth, I would prevent any germs from going in my mouth that would have gotten in there in the time I had been talking.

I mean think about it. If I didn't open my mouth to talk, the germs in the air wouldn't be able to get in. Less germs equals no getting sick. It was the perfect plan. It didn't matter that I was breathing in the same air through my nose the whole day. According to my PANDAS Brain, it only mattered if they got in my mouth.

So, I did it. I stopped talking in the school building unless a teacher asked me a question, in which case I obviously had to answer. Other than that, I figured I could get away with nodding, shaking my head, or shrugging my shoulders as answers to everyone else's questions. And that strategy actually worked… for like two classes.

No one knew what was wrong with me. *I* didn't even know what was wrong with me. All of a sudden, the girl that my classmates had been going to school with since Pre-K stopped talking. Even I have to admit that I would have been pretty weirded-out. Some of them resorted to coming up to me and asking why I was being so quiet, and I would just shrug and stand there until they went away. Others started asking around the grade in secret to see if anyone knew what was up. No one had any ideas. It was horribly embarrassing for me, but I really did think that I was doing myself a favor in the long run.

So, my fifth-grade year was spent pretty much just avoiding talking to anyone while I was in the school. I figured that as long as I didn't open my mouth, my chances of getting sick would be drastically reduced, and I was willing to try anything to avoid getting sick.

I'm sure it baffled my classmates that I would not talk inside the building, and I was my regular self outside, but I couldn't think about that. I was protecting myself from the potential of vomiting, which had been my number one priority since second grade.

I couldn't tell if my teachers really noticed at first that suddenly all of my questions stopped and my class participation came to a standstill, but soon they started deducting points from my participation grade. When that started to happen, my mom went in and met with my teachers, explaining the situation as best as possible. Admittedly, it must have sounded pretty far-fetched. If I wasn't the one going through it, I probably would have thought that I was just trying to make excuses for being a lazy student. Most of the teachers didn't get it, but they tried to be accommodating anyway, which was all I could ask.

If at any time I needed to open my mouth (like if a teacher called on me despite my mom explaining my situation to them), my heart would start beating faster and I mumbled, trying my hardest to not open my mouth any longer or wider than absolutely necessary. I hoped that opening my mouth as little as possible would reduce the number of germs that got in. If I couldn't avoid letting them in in order to talk to a teacher, I figured I might as well try to decrease the amount of contamination that had to happen.

Then, after I spoke, I would begin the ritual that my brain had thought up for such occasions: I would take all of the saliva in my mouth and push it into the space between my lips and front teeth then strain it through my teeth. I know it's gross. But the idea behind it was that by straining it through my front teeth I was leaving the germs that had gotten in my saliva in the area between my teeth and my lips, which was much better than having all of those germs just floating around in my mouth.

I repeated this ritual as many times as I felt it was necessary, and it quickly became a hassle and an embarrassment. First of all, I could do it up to ten times after opening my mouth once, and you wouldn't think so, but after about three times the process actually started to get painful.

On top of that, I felt the need to try to hide my face from my classmates whenever I did the ritual, because once I had caught a look at myself in a mirror in the middle of a "mouth-cleansing", and I realized that the resulting face was less than flattering. I was also extremely nervous that my classmates would hear me moving the saliva around in my mouth and would think that I was disgusting, so I tried to only spit-strain when the rest of the class was being fairly noisy. Obviously, this required a lot of planning to get the timing right, and sometimes I would do the proper amount of straining after opening my mouth to answer one question only to have the teacher call on me again to answer another as soon as I was done, resulting in me having to begin the process all over again.

Sometimes the "mouth-cleansing" even spilled over into the next class period because I hadn't had enough time in the previous one to finish it to my satisfaction. It didn't take long at all before I was tired of the dumb ritual; but I kept doing it, believing that it would protect me from germs.

Meanwhile, my friends adjusted to the new, way quieter me fairly quickly. They were a little confused at first, but eventually I guess they kind of figured that it was something that had to do with

OCD. Unlike the rest of my grade, they all knew about what had happened in second grade, although we never talked about it. So they probably just wrote it off as something related to that, even though they couldn't figure out the connection between the two.

Without making it into a big deal, my close friends altered how they talked to me in the school building. They stopped asking open ended questions that required a verbal answer and started asking me yes or no questions instead. That way I could nod or shake my head as the response, instead of opening my mouth to actually answer them.

I honestly cannot describe how amazing it was for them to stick with me even though I was acting really weird. I knew they didn't really understand it, because I couldn't even understand it, but they tried to make sense of it all the same. I'll be grateful for them for the rest of my life.

My twin brothers were toddlers at this time, and unfortunately, they got sick quite a bit. They were like germ magnets or something, and I felt that they contaminated the house, making it just as unsafe for me as school was. So I did the only thing I could think of to protect myself– whenever they got sick and vomited I locked myself in my room for two weeks, only coming out to leave for school and going back in as soon as I got home.

While I quarantined myself, I had to get creative to pass the time alone in my room. Once, I watched all of the seasons of *That*

70's Show on my IPod Touch. Other times, I did homework all day and tried to get ahead on schoolwork. I just couldn't leave my room. My parents had to bring me my meals, and because I didn't have a phone, the only way I could communicate with them while I was in my room was to email them from my IPod Touch.

And I don't know if anyone else has ever tried this, but just so you know, if you keep all of the doors closed and just sit in your room all day, it doesn't take long for it to get very hot. But the thought of getting sick was too terrifying, so I would wait out the week in my room until I thought the germs in the house had dissipated.

When I decided it was finally safe to come out of my room, I wouldn't talk in the house at all for at least another week. The only way I would be able to speak in the house was if I had a cup of water right next to my mouth. The "logic" was that if I spoke for only as long as it would have taken me to take a sip of water, the same number of germs would get into my mouth as if I was drinking water out of a cup, which I couldn't avoid doing. I figured that if I had to open my mouth, I would be safer if I pretended I was taking a sip of water. Then my mouth would be open in just the same way as it would be whenever I drank water, and no unnecessary germs would get in. If I had anything big to tell my mom I would ask her to meet me in the backyard where I could safely talk to her.

Eventually, the cup ritual stopped being just for after my brothers had gotten sick, and I finally ventured out of my room. It became something that had to be done every day, every single time I talked in the house. Without the safety of a water cup in front of my mouth, all of my talk inside my house stopped, and the only place I could freely talk was outside. This meant that I couldn't have friends over to my house, because I wouldn't be able to talk to them without them noticing me putting the cup of water to my mouth whenever I spoke. I had to walk around all the time carrying my cup with me in case my parents would ask me a question. If I didn't have the cup with me when someone asked me a question, they would have to wait for me to run and get it before I could answer their question.

The whole thing got old really fast, but I felt completely powerless against it. There were a few days every now and then when I would get particularly frustrated at my inability to talk in the house, and I would just talk inside because I was fed up with being OCD's prisoner. But those rare bursts of courage only lasted a few minutes, and after saying a few words without my cup I lost my nerve.

I only remember two specific incidents from sixth grade year. The first was that I found out that one of the funniest and most-liked teachers of our grade also suffered from anxiety. We had a really good relationship to begin with, but once she told me that we shared that trait it was like we just had more to bond over.

One day, she took me aside and told me that if I ever started to feel too anxious during class, she would allow me to leave and walk around for a while to calm down. After hearing about the "no talking in the school building" situation, she stopped calling on me and never pressured me to do anything that would upset me. She even skipped over me when the class went down the rows reading passages from the textbook unless I told her that I was up for reading (which rarely ever happened). She was definitely one of the most understanding and sympathetic teachers I've ever had, and I can only hope that she knows how much I appreciate everything she did for me. She was one of the first teachers ever that I knew wasn't judging me for my response to my anxiety; she was on my side.

I looked forward to her class every day, and it quickly became the class I felt safest in. Even though my classmates made confused faces every time she skipped over me to read, she and I would share an understanding glance, and what the others thought didn't bother me. Sometimes Mrs. H and I would plan days when I would force myself to read when it was my turn, and on those days, I could tell my teacher was proud that I was fighting back against my anxiety. It meant a lot to finally have a teacher that I was sure didn't think I was crazy because I couldn't talk in the school building, and I could tell that she cared more about me than the lesson plan.

The second thing that I remember about sixth grade was something that happened during a therapy session with Mrs. H that I think still affects me today. I didn't realize the impact it had on me at the time, but it definitely played a role in shaping my behaviors down the line.

I sat in my usual chair across from her and my mom. We were discussing the ways in which my anxiety was limiting my life, specifically not talking in the school building, when my therapist asked me a question that had never occurred to me before.

"Do you think that people may think that you're a…" she leaned forward, "…bitch?" she whispered. "For not talking to them, I mean."

This was a whole new idea to me. What if people thought that I had turned into the biggest brat ever when I wasn't talking to them in school? I never meant to make anyone feel bad or think that I didn't like them, and until that moment I never even thought that my silence was doing anything except protecting me from germs and maybe making my classmates think I was a little weird. But now I thought about it and the notion terrified me.

I had no intention of being rude to my classmates, but of course, I also had no way of telling them what I was actually trying to do. There was no way I could try to explain what was going on without sounding like an absolute lunatic, and I found myself kind of stuck between looking snobby and looking crazy. I was just trying to protect myself. I didn't really take into account how others would interpret it.

Ever since Mrs. H asked me that one question, I have never been able to stop thinking about what other people think about me when I am unable to talk to them, and I strongly believe that the proposition played a role in me developing such horrible social anxiety a little later on in my life. After that, instead of not taking into account what others thought of my silence, it became all I could focus on. It ended up being just another thing to obsess over.

By far, the year I remember most from elementary school is seventh grade, the year before I started high school. I had waited so long to get to be the "top dog," the oldest grade in the school, and it was finally my time. I took it upon myself to make it the best year yet, no matter what stood in the way. In my case, it was the fact that I couldn't talk inside the school building.

So, I made up my mind that I would talk for the whole year despite how much I felt I was putting myself in danger of getting sick. I was so tired of all my days of complete silence in school that I gathered enough nerve to get me through the year. I was so fed up that I almost didn't care that I was destining myself to get sick. I just wanted to be myself again.

Mind you, I didn't talk a lot, but it was a huge step after three years. Obviously, some days were better than others, and it was really difficult to push myself to talk, even if it was just to say one word. I felt like I had to physically force my mouth open, working against everything in my head telling me to keep my mouth shut. A lot of other factors also played into how talkative I was, and really my amount of talking varied hour to hour.

For example, on days when kids got sick at school I was quieter than normal, and my spit-straining ritual made a huge comeback. In the weeks after one of my classmates got sick I would avoid them like the plague and hold my breath whenever they passed by, hoping to steer clear of catching the same germs. It didn't matter to my PANDAS Brain that germs don't stick around for that long and that's not how that works. In my head it made sense, and as far as I knew it worked.

Even with all of the components that played into how much or how little I could talk every day, I still got through seventh grade and graduated with my peers. I made a lot of good memories in that year, and though I still had to have my cup to talk at home, it ended up being one of the best years I've had since I was diagnosed with PANDAS in second grade. I felt like I was finally on the path to taking my life back, and I couldn't have been more ready for high school.

Chapter 10

Eighth Grade: New School, New Worries

High school is a completely different animal and going to an all-girl high school after nine years at a co-ed school was like culture shock. When I started eighth grade, I was a nervous minnow in a tank full of huge fish, but I was determined to make it work. The main thing that had me so confident that I could escape unscathed was the fact that I could actually talk in this school building. This was a completely different school at an entirely different location, and it was like my PANDAS Brain reset.

At my elementary school, I had been there long enough to witness some students get sick while on that campus, but at this new school I hadn't been there for enough time to see anyone vomit, so I could write it off as a safe place. It was especially pleasant because this was the first year that my high school classmates would spend with me, and I was able to interact with them normally. I was starting over with a clean slate, and my biggest priority was to make a good impression– not to be the weird kid who didn't say anything.

It was so liberating to be able to talk at school for the first time in years, and obviously I was excited to see what the year would bring.

The first few weeks of eighth grade were pretty good. Nothing exciting really happened apart from me realizing that I hated algebra. I tried my best to balance my schoolwork and expand my social circle, making sure to show everyone the personality that I had to keep to myself for so many years. I felt like high school would be a good opportunity to redeem myself in front of the people that had gone to elementary school with me, and all of my classmates that I had never met before never needed to know about my mental issues.

But, with about two weeks left of the first quarter, I got sick (for your innocence, I'll spare you the details). I wasn't vomiting, so I counted my blessings– but I was really sick. It was like a horrible GI bug that just wouldn't go away. I ended up having to stay home from school for two weeks (one of those being a week of exams) lying on the sofa, because if I stood up I blacked out. I lost quite a bit of weight, and my mom told me that I looked like a "limp kitchen towel."

For a long time, we couldn't get in to see a doctor, and we found ourselves debating whether or not I needed to be hospitalized. With my sickness not letting up and me missing a massive amount of school, when we were finally able to get a doctor's appointment we leapt at the opportunity. The doctor diagnosed me with Adeno Virus and pneumonia– not an ideal combo. But knowing what I had meant that we could finally start treatment, and hopefully I would be able to go back to school fairly quickly.

When I was okay enough try to go to school, I started with half days, going straight to the guidance counselor's office where I would copy notes, takes tests and quizzes, and eventually make up all of my exams. After making up two weeks' worth of work in about a week I was cleared to rejoin my classmates in the regular school day.

I still remember the first lesson I had as soon as I finished in the guidance office. I had just taken my last make-up test, and I was more than ready to go back to class and get back into the usual swing of things instead of coming into school at ten o'clock, taking three exams, then going back home. So I walked down the hall to English class and sat in my desk, trying to figure out what we were even talking about. My classmates greeting me immediately, because to be honest, I had been gone so long they probably thought I was dead. They all wanted to know where I had been and what had happened. And in the middle of all of their questions it hit me.

Have you ever wondered what it feels like to be hit by one hundred eighteen-wheelers? The feeling that I had at that moment is exactly how I imagine getting bulldozed by one hundred big rigs would feel, because that's when I realized that I couldn't answer my classmates. My PANDAS Brain wouldn't allow it.

School was most likely the place that I had gotten the virus that had incapacitated me for two weeks, and I couldn't put myself at risk of getting sick like that again. Next time I got that sick, vomiting would probably also be part of the package. I needed to keep my mouth shut so the germs wouldn't get in again. School was no longer a safe place for me– it was just another no-talking zone, another place where I had to keep my guard up at all times in order to protect myself.

At that moment, all of my hopes and expectations for the five years ahead of me were shattered. I couldn't talk in the school building. In my eighth-grade year. The year when I was supposed to embrace a fresh start with only a few people who had gone to elementary school with me and witnessed my silence. I was going to be the funny girl in every class, inserting witty comments whenever I felt it was necessary. My whole grade was going to know me as the fun one, and people would be excited to have classes with me.

Nope. Not anymore. That vision was over. Because now, I had to accept the fact that I was going to have to nod and shake my head instead of speaking and the fact that I would be known as the weird, quiet one, not the fun one. I felt so stupid that I hadn't seen this coming. And what better time for this to occur to me than in my first regular class in two weeks?

Needless to say, that was a terrible class. My classmates talked to me and included me in their conversations, expecting me to be the person they had met at the beginning of the school year, talking and laughing like usual. But obviously I couldn't do that. Instead, I sat in my desk and avoided eye contact why simultaneously trying to keep my face from showing my overwhelming sense of panic. And I passed the rest of the day like that. People started noticing immediately, asking if I was okay or why I was being so quiet. I just shrugged in reply and hoped that they wouldn't try to make any further conversation.

Weeks went by like that, and then months in a similar fashion. It didn't even take one week for everyone in my grade to know that there was something wrong with me, but no one knew what it was. Amazingly fortunate for me, my friends understood just like they had in elementary school and took it in stride, altering the way they talked to me into yes or no questions again instead of making it into an ordeal. But no one else was that understanding.

People started asking me why I was being so quiet. When that didn't elicit an answer other than a shrug, my classmates started actively trying to make me talk. Some would gather around me in groups and talk to me about how quiet I was, so that the entire rest of the class would hear. Others would ask me questions that were purposely altered so that I couldn't just shake my head yes or no in response with the sole desire to get me to talk back to them.

Still there were others who apparently took it upon themselves to break my silence like it was their own personal goal. They would flat out ask me to talk, evidently thinking that would somehow free me from whatever had suddenly made me so quiet. Some people took a simpler route and went up to my friends and blatantly asked them what was wrong with me. My friends somehow always made up excuses to try to get them to leave me alone, but it didn't stop the majority of people from harassing me about my silence.

For the rest of eighth grade, I sat through every class with at least one person asking me a question that was not a yes or no question, to which I would just shrug, because I didn't know what else to do. I couldn't go one day without someone telling me to "just say something" so that they could go on with their day and feel like they had accomplished something by getting me to say one word.

It only took about two days for the whole routine to get old. Soon, I dreaded going to school for two main reasons: I didn't have the freedom to talk there, and people made a point to make my silence a big deal. I also had the ever-present dread that a teacher would call on me at some point in the day, and I would have to answer. Then my meticulous spit-filtering ritual ensued, which was a pain to complete and try to hide at the same time. And if all of that wasn't enough, I still constantly worried about what Mrs. H had said about people thinking that I was a "stuck up bitch" for not talking to them.

I didn't want all of these new people to think I was a horrible person because I suddenly stopped talking to them. I became very aware of not only how they must have interpreted my sudden one-eighty on an attitude level, but also how crazy it must have looked to my classmates.

It didn't take long at all for my silence to take a mental toll. Every day I felt so alone for the seven hours I spent at school, because isolation seemed like the best way to avoid getting sick. I couldn't think about how everyone thought I had lost my mind, and I couldn't think about how I wasn't going to reach my full potential in high school because I couldn't communicate like everyone expected me to– like I wanted to.

Being surrounded by people, but not being able to say anything is a really weird experience, and it was only magnified by my classmates prodding me to talk, not knowing what my issue was. I understood their confusion. I didn't really fully understand the reasoning myself. But I had to believe that my silence would keep me safe, because if I didn't, I wouldn't have been able to even go to school. I would have never left my room, and I surely would have just come up with other ways to cope or "protect" myself against the potential illnesses that were all around me.

So, I stayed quiet and reentered my silent prison every morning at 7:20. Apart from the five friends that sat with me at lunch, everyone kind of ignored me unless they were trying to get me to say something. And that's the way I wanted it. I tried my best to ignore the weird looks and the things I knew people were saying about me behind my back, because I needed this silence just to come to school in the morning and function like everyone else.

The whole, entire school year passed like that. The whole thing. I kept myself in a constant state of denial that there wasn't anything wrong with the current arrangement and pretended to not notice my unhappiness, even though it was only my first year of high school. By the time the year finally ended, I felt nothing but relief that summer had arrived.

Chapter 11

The Summer of Eighth Grade Year

I was so done with school by the time summer came around that I decided to make the most out of my vacation and accompany my aunt and her family to Callaway Gardens in Georgia. Two nights before I left for the trip, I made plans to sleep over at my friend Gabby's house. We ordered Chinese food for dinner, which I had only recently started eating again after extensive work with my therapist, then went out for a movie. On the way back to her house from the theater I became aware of the fact that I was feeling… not right. I didn't want to say anything, though, because I didn't think it would be a big deal– and we were going to her house to make JiffyPop! I had never done that before.

But by the time we made the popcorn it was exceedingly clear to me that I would not be able to eat it. I decided to wait it out a few more hours and see if I felt better before bed. I was hoping that what I was feeling was the usual jitters I felt every time I slept away from home. Sleep overs always intensified my anxiety, no matter where I was. Eventually the feeling would always pass, so I held onto the hope that tonight the same thing would happen.

However, bed time rolled around, and I knew that I needed to go home. It was around midnight when I went into the bathroom and called my mom. She obviously didn't answer because she was asleep, but I panicked. I figured I was just being a bit dramatic, so I tried to go back to bed. A few minutes later I went back to the bathroom, though, because the last thing I wanted to do was get vomit all over Gabby's room. I called both parents this time, knowing that it would be really bad if I couldn't get one of them to come get me. I could tell that I was getting closer to the time that I would be getting sick, and my panic was getting worse every second.

If it was going to happen (and by this point I knew it was) I at least wanted to be home, where I was most comfortable. By putting myself in an environment that I was familiar with it would have eliminated all of the other anxiety about getting sick. I wouldn't have to worry about the embarrassment of telling Gabby, I wouldn't gross her out, so she never had me over again, and most importantly, my parents knew how to calm me down. I would only have one thing that I would have to worry about instead of multiple– I would just have to get the vomiting over with. I needed to get home. I needed my parents to answer, and I needed them to come get me so I could be home when all of this went down.

By the time I finally got a hold of my parents I had called my mom's phone, my dad's phone, and the house phone at least five times each. I ended up having to call and wake up my dad in order to ask him to give my mom the phone so I could explain my predicament to her. She came and got me immediately, and she knew I was seriously freaked out as soon as she saw me. I hopped in the car and started trying to calm myself, still holding onto the hope that I wasn't actually sick, but instead felt so horrible because I was actually just having a panic attack.

Lo and behold, about 5-8 minutes away from my house, I threw up all over the front seat of the car. My mom had to pull over in the middle of an expressway we were driving on (which, thank God, was empty) in order to make sure I was okay. She helped me out of the car, and I sat in the middle of the emergency lane of the expressway, completely shocked about what had just happened. I was so shocked, in fact, that I just kept asking my mom if this was a dream.

What would happen now? What kind of rituals would I have to do? How could I protect myself from having this happen again? What if I got sick again later on in the night? How would we clean that out of the car? I was so convinced that this was just another one of those nightmares about me getting sick that had become so familiar over the years. But no. My mom assured me that it was real life.

The panic immediately started to set in that there was a chance that I could vomit again. I had gotten sick once that night, and it could easily happen again. Instead of telling myself that I wouldn't get sick again, I tried to be realistic and submit myself to the fact that I probably would. I started to tell myself over and over that there was nothing I could do about it, and if I really thought about it, getting sick wasn't even so bad. It would be over in a second, and tomorrow I would feel a lot better. (I don't know why I thought this reasoning would suddenly calm me if it hadn't worked for the past seven plus years, but I didn't have any other ideas.)

When we finally made it back to the house, I got straight into the bathtub and just sat there, still trying to wrap my head around what had just happened. I'll spare you the rest of the details of that night, but in a nutshell, I was so scared that I didn't want to sleep, and it took me about an hour to actually drift off, even with my mom next to me. I felt like my thoughts were running around in circles, and the worry that I would vomit again made it hard for me to quiet my mind.

The next day was the day before I left for Georgia, and I was still freaking out about it. What if it happened again while I was away with my cousins? My mom wouldn't be there to calm me down in the way she does, and I didn't think I would be able to handle it. My aunt and her family made it clear that I was still welcome to accompany them despite what had happened the night before, but I was really hesitant.

Somehow, my mom convinced me to go, assuring me that I would be fine. On the ride to their house the next morning, I sat in the third row of seats in my mom's car, in the seat farthest away from where I had thrown up. I wouldn't talk, wouldn't open my mouth, wouldn't take a full breath. I pressed my face up against the window and tried my best to avoid as many germs as possible.

By the time I arrived back at home after my vacation, it was clear that my PANDAS Brain had placed more restrictions on me. No more Chinese food. That's what I had eaten on the night I got sick, and I had already had a bad experience with it in the past. I should have seen that as a warning; it was dumb for me to have been so stupid as to let my therapist convince me that it was okay to eat it again. Well, never again. (I have not eaten Chinese food to this day, and I don't see myself eating it in the future.)

And I could no longer go to the movies. The fact that I had seen a movie at the movie theater the night I got sick made them connected. I felt the need to hold my breath whenever I just saw pictures of the characters that were in the movie I had seen that night with Gabby, and I still do to this day. As soon as it was clear that this was one of the rules that resulted from that night, my mom begged me to go see a movie with her, because she wanted me to be completely free from my PANDAS Brain. I appreciated her intentions, but I knew that the chance of getting to the point of ever stepping in a movie theater again was slim to none.

Another rule associated with that night is that I felt inclined to hold my breath whenever we passed the place on the expressway where I had gotten sick. This doesn't really sound so bad, but it actually really was. The amount of time on the expressway that I had to hold my breath got longer and longer the farther we got from the occurrence of the actual incident, and I passed that spot everyday going to and from school. I had to hold my breath so long before and after passing the spot that my vision usually went black, and I got lightheaded. But I felt it was necessary to not let the germs in.

I never felt like these rules really affected my daily life that much, though. I could avoid Chinese food and movie theaters easily enough. I managed to convince my friends that I hate Chinese food instead of telling them that I'm not "allowed" to eat it. And I always managed to make up excuses to get out of going to see movies with my friends. I felt like I was missing out a little bit when they went out to the movies without me, but it was worth it if I was protecting myself from getting sick… right?

The only rule that I felt really impacted me was that from that point on I was not allowed to talk in the car that I had gotten sick in. I couldn't sit in the seat I had been in when I vomited, and I certainly couldn't open my mouth or talk. There was no getting around it. My PANDAS Brain told me that the same germs that had made me sick on that night would still be in the car, and if I opened my mouth, no matter how long, I would end up sick again. Upon entering the car, I put my face as close to the window I could and tried to breathe as little as possible.

The circle of places where I was allowed to talk was progressively getting smaller and smaller. My mom's car and school were no longer safe places, and my house wasn't really safe either. My brothers were young and were often getting sick, so I was always on edge, knowing that it was only a matter of time before they got me sick too.

I kept my guard up all the time, believing that my rituals were the only thing between me and vomiting. That was probably the first summer that I realized that my freedom was shrinking. I didn't realize the gravity of the situation until a few years later, but I could feel it happening. And I didn't know how to stop it.

Chapter 12

Ninth Grade: Disenchanted

At that point, I was one hundred percent adamant that I would not talk in my mom's car. There would be no compromising– it wouldn't happen. Dr. H, on the other hand, had other ideas. Obviously, at my next appointment she found out about the whole "throw up in the car" incident and all of my new rituals that resulted from it. And within twenty minutes she had determined that I was indeed going to talk in the car. That day, she decided, we were going to do an exposure in which I faced the thing that terrified me the most.

Despite my protests, she grabbed *Where the Wild Things Are* for me to read when we got into the car, and we made our way downstairs. I jumped into the seat furthest away from the passenger seat and sat there with my arms crossed, trying to burn holes into Mrs. H's head with my eyes. Not only did that not work, but she also told me that I needed to sit in the same seat I had been in when I had gotten sick.

It didn't take me long to realize that there was no way I could get out of this. I couldn't think of any way I could get her to stop doing this to me. So, after a few minutes of her trying to convince me that everything would be okay, I climbed into the front seat and sat there with my knees by my chest without saying a word. Mrs. H tried to get me to talk, but I made it very clear that I had no intention of reading that book.

Just getting into the car had been too much for me, and I thought she was absolutely insane for making me sit in the same seat I had been in when I got sick. But now she handed me the book and waited for me to open my mouth. I could feel my heart beating out of my chest, because I knew I couldn't possibly do this. If I spoke inside the car, it was a sure bet that I would get sick again. All of the germs that had made me sick were still in the car, exactly where I was sitting. I didn't even feel comfortable in the third row of seats farthest away from the scene of the incident. How did she expect me to be able to do this?

Pure terror doesn't even begin to describe the feeling I felt in that moment. I was absolutely powerless against getting sick if I opened my mouth in there. All of the time I spent trying to protect myself would mean nothing. I would be throwing it all away.

After about ten minutes of sitting in silence, Mrs. H had the idea for me to open the window to read the book, because the air flow would make me less nervous about the germs being stagnant in the passenger seat. By this time, I was just plain mad at her, so I decided to take her up on her offer. I opened the window.

And I climbed through it. I sat myself down right there in the window with my butt hanging out toward the sidewalk and my head sticking up over the roof of the car. The only part of me that was actually still in the car was my feet.

I don't think that's really what Mrs. H had in mind when she suggested that I open the window, but frankly I didn't care. I started reading the book as quickly as I could without opening my mouth, which is actually more difficult than you would think. But eventually, I finished it, and we walked back up to her office where I refused to even look at her.

I felt so betrayed– I had told her that I didn't feel comfortable doing the exposure, but we did it anyway. I know it sounds like a really stupid thing to get so upset about, but anxiety isn't rational. It made me feel like not only was I fighting against my OCD at that point, but I was also fighting against her when she was supposed to be the one helping me. Why did I even have to re-learn to talk in the car? I was perfectly content just sitting silently in the backseat. I didn't really care about not being able to talk in school either. My friends were the only ones I really cared about, and they were extremely accommodating.

It wasn't even important to me anymore that I didn't talk in the car or at school. The exposures caused me too much anxiety, and there were too few results for it to be worth it. But the part that got me the most was that I thought Mrs. H would understand that. I thought she would understand that she was pushing me too far this time.

Wasn't she supposed to understand what I was going through? Of all the people in my life, I thought that she would have been the first one to understand what I was feeling. But instead, I felt like she had gotten too wrapped up in seeing results and had lost sight of my best interest. The amount of panic that exposure had caused me didn't seem justified.

That was the last time I ever saw Mrs. H. After that session, I refused to go to any appointments with her and ended up swearing off therapy completely. I told my mom that I was "taking a break" after that last appointment, but I never had any intentions of going back. And I never did. Whenever my mom would bring up therapy for the next year it would end in a fight, because she tried to get me the help she knew I needed, and I refused it every time.

But to be honest, I had never felt like I benefitted from therapy anyway. I was frustrated that I had been trying for so many years to make myself better using therapy, and all it did was make me anxious and grumpy. I was tired of being scared of such a stupid thing that everyone else could handle easily. So, I surrendered myself to the fact that my silence in school, at home, and in the car was something that would never change.

I didn't see the point in trying to find another therapist like my mom suggested. As far as I was concerned, I could be my own therapist, because that's what I felt I had been doing even when I was in therapy. The tools that my therapist gave me never worked, and I had to devise my own ways to cope. I didn't need a therapist to tell me how to live my life– I was fine with the way it was. So, the answer was no. I would not go back to therapy no matter what anyone tried to tell me.

When school started up again, I still remained firm in my resolve to be anti-therapy. It actually kind of took a weight off my shoulders– no more appointments and no more of Mrs. H trying to convince me to talk at school. I got more than enough of that from my peers throughout the school day. I didn't have to worry about my silence in the house and in my mom's car being unhealthy, because there was no one there to tell me that it was limiting my life.

Without a therapist, I could stay in denial that there wasn't anything wrong with the way I was living. My coping techniques had gotten me this far, so why should I listen when someone tried to tell me to change them just because I wasn't living my best life? If it ain't broke don't fix it, right?

Freshman year passed in much the same way as eighth grade year did. Other students tried to convince me or "trick" me into talking, and all I could do in response was nod yes or no. When people asked me anything other than a yes or no question all I could do was shrug and hope they didn't think I was being rude.

I eventually resorted to avoiding eye contact so they wouldn't ask me questions and smiling if they ever did, all the while hoping I didn't lose my mind. Fortunately, my friends continued to be understanding, and the course work for the year wasn't too overwhelming. So, ninth grade year eventually drew to a close, and my silence in the car, at school, and in the house continued. Just like every other year, I was so relieved when summer finally arrived.

Chapter 13

Sophomore Slump

I had wanted a job since I was little, and that summer I decided to get one. I applied at a frozen yogurt shop three minutes from my house, and I spent the majority of my summer there, feeling more and more independent every paycheck I got. The job helped to distract me from the impending school year, which I had heard was the hardest year academically at my high school. People kept on telling me how heavy the workload was and warned me that everyone in my grade would kind of go crazy during the year because their bodies would go through so many changes. So obviously I was really nervous about going back to school.

When school let back in at first, I did pretty well. Everyone still thought I was weird because I wouldn't talk, and that upset me. But I thought I was kind of used to it. A few days into the school year, though, I got my first "omen," I guess you could say, that the year was going to be really rough when I met my guidance counselor for the first time. Everyone in the grade has the same guidance counselor and gets a meeting with her/him during the first quarter of the school year in order for her/him to "get to know you." (Because apparently you can really get to know someone in five minutes.)

So, I had my pass, and I walked up to her office and sat down, expecting this interaction to be easier for me than the ones I had with my peers. I still had to get over the fact that I was in the school building, but it had been a rule since eighth grade year that the only reason I would speak in the school was if an adult/teacher asked me a question. Much to my chagrin, she qualified, so I had to talk to her.

We got through general introductions, and she asked me if there was anything else I thought she should know about me in order to help me throughout the year. I hesitated for a second before saying "I have OCD," because no one at school, outside of my group of friends, knew. I wasn't comfortable with telling anyone about my situation, but I figured it would probably be safe to tell her considering she was supposed to help me stay sane during the school year.

She looked nonchalantly at me and said, "Don't we all?" I was so taken aback for a second that what she said didn't even sink in. Then I realized that she thought I was telling her "I have OCD" just like people do when they're neat-freaks and think that's what OCD is.

My *guidance counselor* had just assumed that I wasn't talking about the actual mental illness but was just throwing the phrase "I'm OCD" around like it just meant everything had to be neat and tidy. She hadn't even given any thought to the possibility that I could *actually* have OCD and have struggled with it for more than half my life. I had to literally tell her that I actually was diagnosed with OCD before she realized that I wasn't kidding, and not thirty seconds later, I was on my way back to class.

Before, I had never really given any thought to the fact that people say "Oh, I'm OCD about that" or "I'm so OCD" every single day when they're just talking about needing everything to be organized. But after that incident, I realized how often it happened and how normal it was for someone who doesn't have OCD to say that they do because they think OCD just means that you want everything to be "just right." And I couldn't help but get really upset about that.

The last nine years of my life had been nothing but pure hell because of the obsessions and compulsions and never-ending rituals that came with OCD. By throwing around the term OCD like that, people were minimizing the fact that it's an actual disorder that has actual consequences that don't always include awesome organization skills. I'd spent hours crying in my bed because I was too scared to encounter the germs outside of my room. I'd gone to more therapy sessions than I could count to try to "fix" myself, and nothing had worked. But apparently people thought OCD had no results more serious than slight irritation when your page tabs don't line up.

After that, it didn't take me long at all to realize that all of my worries over the summer were well-warranted. In the midst of all of these new realizations and the new insane amount of schoolwork, I suddenly found myself struggling again with my anxiety and OCD, adding new rituals to my routine every day. But that wasn't even the worst part. The worst part was that suddenly I was extremely depressed.

It seemed to hit me all at once that anxiety and OCD are incurable. I realized that I would struggle with it my whole life, regardless of how hard I tried to leave it in my past. It quickly got to the point where I started to really question if it was even worth it for me to go on living if this was how the rest of my life would be– nothing but anxiety and constant depressive thoughts that made me hate myself. I knew I was doomed to live a life of continuous bombardments of mental health issues, and I didn't see a point of living, because the way I saw it, that wasn't life.

I mean, I wasn't ever going to be able to make a difference in the world, because my life was consumed by anxiety, so what was the point? I was just going to suffer the entire time, hating every second of every day. And at the end of the day, nothing would ever come of it. We all die sometime, and if my life wasn't going to have an impact on others, then why did it matter when it happened?

I was consumed by an overwhelming sense of hopelessness. I knew it would never get better, and I knew that I would never get to live like everyone else. They didn't have to worry about talking in a school building or playing outside at P.E. They didn't have to be scared of vanilla pudding or pretzels. But I did. And I always would.

Didn't I deserve a break? I felt like for the past ten years I had to try fifteen times harder than other people just to get out of bed in the morning, because my brain did nothing but try to talk me out of going out into the germy world. I had to worry about the stupid things that no one else would even think about and do rituals that I knew were illogical just to lessen my anxiety. For once, I just wanted silence in my head. I thought I deserved that much.

My mom could tell that something was wrong, so she pulled me aside one day and said that she had found a therapist here in New Orleans that specializes in OCD that thought she could help me. I agreed for the sole reason that I just didn't care anymore. I didn't care what happened to me, and I really didn't care who tried to make me normal. I didn't care that I would never know what it's like to not worry about everything or obsess over stupid things. And I didn't care that my life wasn't mine anymore. I didn't want to try, because I knew I would never get better. So, what was the point?

I started seeing Dr. C once a week, mostly to appease my mom, who hoped that she would help with my depression as well as my OCD that had overpowered me yet again. She tried to get me to talk in the car, and she actually succeeded in getting me to have a barely-opening-my-mouth-to-speak phone conversation with my mom while I was sitting in the back seat. After about two of these car sessions, I lost my little spark of bravery, though, and my motivation to change the talking-in-the-car situation went with it.

After that, I found every single possible excuse to stay out of the car, and eventually my family ended up getting a new one. So that problem was finally out of my life. But it turned out I had a lot more issues than just that.

It didn't take Dr. C long at all (maybe one appointment) for her to diagnose me with severe depression. It was pretty obvious– I was at such a dark place that I didn't even want to get help anymore. I just wanted it to end. I had lost interest in all the things I used to find fun and pushed my friends and family away.

On top of that, Dr. C diagnosed me with social anxiety, which made me even more unwilling to go anywhere except my house and school. So, my OCD and anxiety made functioning day-to-day difficult, my depression constantly told me things would never get better, and my social anxiety made me scared of everyone I came into contact with. A great mix.

Dr. C tried to help me deal with all of this, but I didn't feel like I was making any progress. And my depression was getting so much worse. Every single day I woke up thinking about how this anxiety that I was constantly feeling would never go away. I was completely powerless against it– I had been for nine years, and I would be for the rest of my life. No one beats mental illness. That's not how it works.

With every day that passed it became increasingly clear to me that the fight I had to put up every day wasn't worth it. I had tried too hard for too long for me to have made so little progress.

If this was how the rest of my life was going to be, I might as well just end it right then and there, because I refused to live like that every single day. The smallest little thing could set me off, and I would be depressed for the next week. Nothing would help, nothing could convince me things were going to get better. And I was frustrated that I didn't even know what my triggers were that catapulted me into a rut I couldn't get out of.

The depression was unlike anything I had ever experienced before. I had grown up hearing people talk about how they were "depressed" when the Icee machine wasn't working or when they dropped food. But this was crazy. There isn't even a way that I could explain it that would do it justice. All of a sudden, I would completely shut down, and even though I could feel it happening, there was nothing I could do about it.

There was just an overwhelming feeling of sadness and pain that I couldn't justify, and it stayed with me all day every day. Instead of having bouts of sadness that would pass, it was like I was living in one giant depressive episode. Sometimes, there wasn't a clear reason for why I felt so horrible. Sometimes, there were obvious triggers.

Either way, the feeling never went away. The feeling that I was turning my wheels and going nowhere, the feeling that I was a burden to the people around me. It was like I couldn't feel anything– not happiness, not excitement, not anything other than sadness. And I didn't want to bring anyone else down with my apparent inability to feel anything or bring myself out of what was going on inside my head.

I figured it would be easier if I just wasn't alive anymore, so I didn't have to feel this way every day and the people around me wouldn't be affected. I wanted to get away from the voices in my head constantly telling me that I wasn't good enough or that I was a disappointment. I needed a break from my toxic inner monologue that made me hate everything about myself with every fiber of my being. I wanted relief from what seemed to be the only thing I could feel: sadness.

I began to literally repulse myself. I loathed every single thing about me– especially my body, and there was not one day that went by where I didn't tell myself how ugly I was. There were so many things that played into this: I looked fat, I had stretch marks, I had cellulite– the list went on and on. I resorted to not looking at my body as much as possible. Because if I happened to catch a glimpse in the mirror, I was disgusted, and the rest of my week would be ruined.

With every thought I had, a self-deprecating comment would follow. It didn't matter what it was. I could make an observation and in the next breath silently yell at myself for making a note of something so obvious. If I failed to make an observation, I was stupid for not noticing what was right in front of me.

If I didn't understand something, my thoughts would immediately go to how stupid I was. If I did understand something, my inner voice would sarcastically congratulate me for being able to understand such a simple piece of information.

And my social anxiety was always a factor, especially at school. The other people in my grade still thought I was weird because I didn't talk. But for the most part, they just let me do my own thing and gave up on trying to get me to speak, because they knew they wouldn't get anywhere. People's opinions of me have always meant more to me than they should, and my depression got worse week by week.

Can you imagine waking up every morning and realizing that you're basically going to a silent jail for seven hours where you always have to be on your guard and know that people are talking about how weird you are? That's what I went through every single week. I started thinking of school as a prison, and every Sunday I would get more depressed knowing that I had to go back the next day.

Music helped make me feel better to a certain extent, and I discovered some of my favorite bands during this time; but music can only take you so far. And weirdly enough, my music actually depressed me even more. For a really weird reason. I would listen to the songs and the lyrics and felt like they all related exactly to what I was going through. And I would think about how much I loved these bands and how amazing they were for helping me get through such a dark time. Then I would realize that they would never know what kind of impact they had on me; they would never know how they brought me back from the edge.

I knew that a lot of the members of the bands I loved so much had gone through similar situations to what I was going through with depression, and I wanted to be able to tell them that they had made such a difference in my life. I wanted them to know that all they had gone through and all the hate they got was worth it, because I appreciated them more than they could ever realize. Their hard times were helping me through mine, and I would forever be grateful for that.

But I knew that I would never be able to tell them any of this. I would never meet them and have the chance to tell them that they were a large part of the reason why I was still alive. And for some reason that thought was almost unbearable. I wanted them to know all the good they did, and it made me upset that I would never be able to tell them.

Just when I thought it couldn't get any worse, one day it occurred to me that low self-esteem is unattractive. And anxiety and depression probably are too. I don't know why I cared so much, but I'd always pictured myself with a significant other at some point, and if anxiety, low self-esteem, and depression are considered unattractive, then I was the ugliest person on earth.

People always tell you, "you have to love yourself before you can love someone else." Well, guess what. I hated myself. How could I love someone if I despised everything about me? It occurred to me that I could try to learn to love myself. But I knew that even if I loved myself other people would still judge me, and that's what I would care about. Because I knew that other people don't care if you love yourself. They'll try to tear you down anyway.

I remember one particular incident where I was trying to talk myself out of doing something. I told myself, "if you do that, you'll hate yourself after." And immediately the first thought that came into my head was "you'll hate yourself anyway." That was the first time that I truly realized that I really did despise myself. I could try to sugar-coat it and say that I was just unhappy with myself at the moment, but in truth I hated myself, and who knew if that would ever change.

So, what was the point of living? I couldn't find one. My parents would eventually get over it if I wasn't there, and it would probably even be better for them, because they wouldn't have to worry about me anymore.

I started thinking of good ways to commit suicide. Pills? Slit wrists? I ran through scenarios in my head and tried to pick out the most painless option. I never fully settled on one method, but it didn't matter; the goal was the same. I wanted to be dead. I didn't want to have to fight against my brain every day anymore. I didn't want to have to deal with the levels of anxiety that came with simple things like talking on the phone or walking into a store. I didn't want to ever have to vomit again. I didn't want to hate everything about myself anymore. I just wanted peace. And suicide felt like the only way to get it.

Cutting myself came into my mind a few times, and every time it seemed more appealing. I wanted to cut myself so I could feel something– even if it was pain. I had felt little to no emotion for the entire year, and I thought maybe I could remind myself that I was still a human with feelings by experiencing the pain that comes with cutting.

I could feel the pressure inside of my body building from my hopelessness and frustrations, and I needed a way to get it out. I wanted cutting to give it all somewhere else to go, because if it stayed with me, at some point it was all going to drive me crazy.

And I hoped it would relieve some tension. I felt so much depression every second of every day that I felt like I needed a way to physically get it out of my body. Like how doctors used to let blood out of patients to get the sickness out of them. I thought maybe cutting myself would give an outlet for the negativity to go somewhere other than inside me.

Truth be told, the only reason I didn't go through with it is because I was too scared. And that just added to my depression. On top of all the other negative traits on the list I had made for myself I had one more to add: I was a coward. I couldn't even work up the courage to try to block out my emotional pain with physical pain? Pathetic.

Every day I thought about self-harm and suicide, and every day I hated myself more. I was the grossest person alive, and no one would miss me if I was gone. In fact, they would probably be relieved. I could try to drown out all of these thoughts with music, but even that wasn't a safe place for me anymore, because it triggered my depression. I was too much of a coward to cut myself, and I knew there wasn't a foolproof way to commit suicide. Even if I got the job done on the first try, I didn't want my parents to have to go through that. No matter how much I told myself that they would get over it quickly because I was nothing but a burden, I couldn't bring myself to do it. I was stuck sixteen feet under rock bottom.

In the midst of all of this, while I was wallowing in my depression pit, it dawned on me that no one knew what I was really going through— not my friends, not my family, not even Dr. C. I couldn't explain to them the pain that I was feeling every day. And how were they supposed to treat me or sympathize with me if they didn't know the severity of the situation inside my head?

I couldn't tell them every thought that came into my head that made me want to end it so they could talk me down. I could try to tell them most of it, and I could go into extreme detail; but I would never be able to tell them everything. There was too much. And I knew that even if I could tell them everything it wouldn't make much of a difference. Their reassurance that I was worthy of living wouldn't mean anything anyway. I was in this alone.

My psychiatrist was (rightfully) worried that therapy wasn't working and asked me to consider going to an institution that specialized in helping people with depression. I told him I'd rather drink bleach.

He wasn't amused.

And neither was I.

I had somehow hit such a low that my *psychiatrist* didn't know what to do with me. He literally didn't know how to make me better, so he was going to institutionalize me. I wasn't a crazy person. I just wanted the pain to end.

And now my psychiatrist couldn't even come up with a way to help me besides put me in an institution and hope for the best. Fantastic. I hadn't thought that I could get any lower, and yet, here I was. Lower than ever and even more aware of how alone I was in my situation. No one knew what was happening in my head every day. So how could I have even hoped that they would know how to help me?

I had never met anyone else who suffered from OCD, so who was I to say that *anyone* understood what I was going through? I was alone in my fight to keep myself alive, because I was the only one who knew just how badly it hurt. Like if you have surgery and you're in a lot of pain, your family can tell you that they "feel for you" or try to sympathize with you; but they don't actually have to go through the pain. Maybe if they knew what it was like they would understand, but they can't feel what you're feeling. So as far as I could tell they just didn't get it.

That's how I felt about everyone in my life– they just didn't get it. If they knew what I had to go through and felt what I felt on a daily basis maybe they would begin to understand. But they couldn't, so they were just people who couldn't sympathize with me telling me that everything would turn out okay.

I think Dr. C began to catch on to the fact that I felt really alone. She organized a group therapy session of me and four other people with OCD who lived in New Orleans, with the goal of showing me how far they had come, even though they struggled just like I did. She wanted to give me hope that I could actually get out of this rut, because I didn't see it ever happening.

I wasn't interested. Even other people with OCD can't know what it feels like to be in my situation. Every case of OCD is different, and even though some cases may share similar traits, no one will be able to grasp the entirety of the disorder's effects on another individual. Someone with OCD can tell me about what they've been through, and I can relate and think about what I would do if I was in their situation. But I wasn't inside their head. I can't know how bad it really was, because what manifests itself on the outside of the body is only about 20% of OCD. The other 80% is mental. For every one symptom/ritual/panic attack/rule that someone else knows about, there are at least fifteen that are unspoken that the person has to deal with alone.

So I wasn't too keen on the group therapy idea. I didn't talk to anyone about what was happening in my head. I didn't even talk to my friends about it. They knew I had OCD and anxiety, but none of them knew I had depression, and certainly no one knew that I was suicidal– not even my sister, and I told her everything.

What were these strangers going to tell me besides "it gets better"? I had heard enough of that and had no doubt in my mind that it doesn't actually get any better. What was the point? I felt like group therapy was just a bunch of people trying to "outdo" each other with how mentally ill they were. Like, "oh, you have anxiety? Well, I have anxiety *and* depression." I had less than zero interest in being a part of it.

When we met I stayed quiet, only mumbling a few words when Dr. C directly asked me to say something. She wanted me to participate, and the other members were really nice, but I didn't see what I would get out of it. I was never going to get better. I had seen multiple therapists and tried uncountable medications over the years, but nothing ever worked. So I resigned myself to the quiet reality that nothing I tried to do to make progress would do anything to make my situation better.

Dr. C ended up telling me the next year when my depression had gotten a little better that the other members of the group had asked her at the time if I would be okay. They could tell I was struggling. If they had asked me that question during a group session my answer would have been "no." No, I wouldn't be okay. The rest of my life was set to be an unending conflict between me and by brain. It probably wouldn't have been long until I ended it.

In fact, one day after group, Dr. C took me aside and made me promise her that I wouldn't do anything, at least until our next appointment. At the time I agreed, but realistically I knew that I couldn't make any promises. I truly didn't know if I would make it to our next appointment; I didn't even know if I would still be alive the next day.

Thankfully, I started taking anti-depressants not long after my first few group sessions, and gradually my depression started to ease up. It was easier for me to function on a daily basis, but even then it was by no means easy. I still thought about self-harm and suicide every day, but it was much more manageable than it had been.

My parents encouraged me to quit my job, believing it added unnecessary stress to go along with my school work and emotional instability. I refused to give it up, though, a feat that I am very proud of many years later. Maybe I wanted to prove to myself that I could do it. Maybe it just took my mind off things for a while. Whatever it was, I somehow managed to keep working throughout all of the ups and downs of my personal life.

My sister had gone away to college for the first time that year, and I really struggled with not being able to talk to her about everything that was going on. Even with the medication, it was just one more factor that gave me a reason to feel depressed. I got even more quiet, even though I already couldn't talk in the car or in the house. This inevitably put a strain on my relationships, and everyone was feeling the effects.

One night, about halfway through the school year, I got a text from one of my best friends telling me that she no longer wanted to be my friend because I was "too negative." To say I was crushed would be an understatement. All of my insecurities came hurtling into my mind, and my depression came with it. "You're too negative" just about summed up some of my greatest fears about my personality flaws. Obviously, the statement had to be true if I had those insecurities about myself and someone confirmed it for me, right?

I've never cried harder in my entire life. I couldn't breathe. My tears filled up my eyes so fast that I couldn't see, but I needed to get out. "You're too negative" swirled around in my brain as I sprinted down the stairs and out the front door. I didn't know what to do or where to go, but I knew that if I stayed in the house, I would find a way to hurt myself.

I ended up collapsing on my driveway. Thank God it was nighttime, so I'm pretty sure none of the neighbors saw me in hysterics sobbing in the front yard, but at the time I didn't care who saw or what they thought. I'd never felt anything like that before. I just wanted to be dead so I couldn't be "too negative" anymore and no one could have anything else bad to say about me again. I hadn't meant for it to affect other people; I thought it was just something that I had to deal with silently. That was the first and hopefully last time I'd had to consciously talk myself down, and I never wanted to feel like that again.

After that, I started filtering everything I said to my friends. I didn't want anyone to think that I was being negative. I didn't want my worst fears about myself to be true. It ended up taking me a while to realize that my real friends would be fine with what I had to say, "negative" or not. Even with that realization, it took me about a year to stop censoring myself, and I still felt an abundance of self-loathing and hatred of people for not being able to understand what I was going through.

I eventually resorted to distancing myself from people as much as possible after realizing that a lot of people were kind of ignorant when it came to the severity of mental illness. Some people acted like mental health issues weren't a problem, and I grew to resent them for it. I hated the fact that some people refuse to believe in the realities of mental illness, simply because it doesn't always manifest itself physically.

I've heard people say that they have opened up to their parents about their struggles with depression only to be told something to the effect of "go pray about it, and God will take care of it."

Guess what. God doesn't just slip you a nice serotonin cocktail and everything is hunky dory. Depression is a chemical imbalance; not something you can pray away. I didn't understand why it was so hard for some people to understand.

Or sometimes when you have something like anxiety, some people will try to tell you to just shake it off, like there's an on and off switch. Do you really think panic attacks would be a thing if I could control whether or not I was having anxiety? Do you really think that I would have chosen to live my life in a constant state of stress?

Still others will tell you to just put it out of your head. …It's called *Obsessive* Compulsive Disorder for a reason. The thoughts don't just leave. If they did, I wouldn't have had all of these issues for the past ten years. If it was that easy, I wouldn't be writing this book.

It frustrated me so much that people could have those types of mentalities about mental health issues, and it made me upset that they would never understand how difficult it is to live with a mental illness unless it happened to them. I lost all of my faith in humanity and readily avoided people whenever possible. They didn't understand me, and for that, I certainly couldn't understand them.

And weeks later, even with all of that on my mind, I still couldn't help but think about how I had lost control of my depression that night my friend texted me about being too negative. My biggest fear became having to go through a depressive episode like that again. If faced with a similar situation, would my depression get as bad as that night when I so strongly felt the urge to seriously hurt myself? And if that happened again, would I be able to stop it?

These were the questions and feelings I brought with me into my junior year of high school. I worked really hard every day to stop the voices in my head from convincing me that I wasn't worthy of living, and I tried to find ways to lessen my dissatisfaction at the prospect of living the rest of my life with depression, OCD, and anxiety. I could only hope that somehow I could get out of the dark place I was in.

Chapter 14

Junior Year: Run a Mile in My Shoes

Going into my junior year, I was still painfully aware of how everyone viewed me as the "weird, quiet one." (Apparently not talking since eighth grade has that effect.) That didn't do anything to help with my social anxiety and depression, and often, I found myself making conscious decisions to seclude myself. I always wanted to sit in the back of the classroom, as far away from anyone else as I could get. I avoided eye contact at all times in an attempt to get out of conversations with my classmates, and I did everything in my power to keep people from talking to me or having to verbally contribute.

One particular incident seemed to harden my resolve to stay quiet on the off chance that I ever felt the urge to speak up. While I was at work, one of my coworkers made a joke that I laughed at. She then took that opportunity to tell me how much she hated my laugh. To her it sounded fake, even though it had been genuine. From that night on, whenever I laughed in her presence, she would mimic my laugh and remind me how much she hated it.

My social anxiety went crazy. What other proof did I need that I didn't have a reason to speak? I mean, why should I talk to anyone other than my friends? Even when I'm outside of school and I talk, I still get made fun of. One of the only times I feel free to talk openly I get judged negatively? No thanks. God knows what would happen when the girls at school ripped me to shreds.

The most talking I could force myself to do was in the house without a cup of water in front of my mouth. I couldn't justify any more than that, and honestly, I felt like that was a big step already. Pretty much the only reason I did even that was just because I was so fed up with not being able to talk in my own house. It had been years since I had spoken for more than a few seconds at a time in my home, and I finally got to the point that I was willing to risk exposing myself to germs.

I hoped there was some truth in my parents' claims that talking in the house didn't increase germ "ingestion" and put what little faith I had into their reassurances that I would be okay. Over the years, my therapists had spent so much time talking about the irrationality of the rule, and even though I knew it was illogical, I still found it hard to make that step.

Other than that development, everything about my talking limitations stayed the same. Admittedly, me talking in the house was a really big deal considering how long I had worked to get to that point. But I felt like I still had a ridiculously long way to go before I could start patting myself on the back.

Anyway, the not-talking thing actually took a backseat to the part of my school career that I hated more than anything: running the mile. I know it sounds incredibly stupid, but the four words "we're running the mile" struck more fear in me than any other schoolwork that year. It's by far one of the dumbest things that has ever caused me such a magnitude of anxiety.

Every quarter since eighth grade, the P.E. classes would run two miles, one at the beginning of the quarter and another at the end. In all, throughout the entire school year we ran eight miles. This really shouldn't have been too big of a problem. But it really was.

We didn't train at all for those mile runs. The P.E. coaches would announce during a random class that we would be running it then or running it next class. So, we always had to be ready to go, even though the only other time most of us had run an entire mile was the last time they forced us to run it during class.

As time went on, I began to dread these runs more and more, for some reason struggled more mentally with them than I had before. I've never been a runner. I'll admit that without any hesitation. But previously, the mile had just been a manageable hurdle to get over during the school day. I ran it and got it over with without a problem.

Something changed near the end of sophomore year. Suddenly, when I heard that we were running the mile I started shaking uncontrollably, and I got so anxious that I felt nauseous. I made it through the rest of the miles of sophomore year, though, and I figured my anxiety about it would clear up over the summer.

I was very wrong. On the day of the first mile, when my coach announced it, I was immediately sent into a frenzy similar to a panic attack. Why? I couldn't put my finger on it, but something about the thought of running it gave me so much anxiety that I wanted to crawl into a corner and cry.

Somehow, I managed to get through that mile. I think it was mostly because I knew I had to. Breaking down in front of everyone in the middle of P.E. class would not have been ideal. I didn't know why I was having these feelings, and I knew that I certainly wouldn't be able to explain them to someone else if my teacher brought me to the guidance counselor.

Now, as I said earlier, I am not in any way, shape, or form a runner. I am not in the least bit athletic; I'm not really gifted in the hand-eye-coordination/physical ability department. So, as I had for the previous three years since eighth grade, I finished with the last stragglers of the group for that first mile. This was nothing new; I was used to finishing close to last, if not last.

But for some reason, this time it hit a nerve. After everyone else finished the mile, they had to sit around and wait until the rest of the class finished. Obviously, some people are more athletic than others and finished running their miles in seven minutes while others finished theirs in ten plus minutes. I had always been part of the latter group. I usually didn't have an issue with it. Running just really wasn't my thing.

For every mile, as my other classmates finished their runs, they gradually began to gather along the edges of the track with nothing else to do but watch the rest of the runners. Sometimes they would cheer for the remaining runners, hoping to send some encouragement, but no matter what, all eyes were on us, the stragglers. This whole practice was nothing but an innocent physical activity performed by members of a group for a grade.

But my social anxiety roared at me. Everyone was looking at me, watching me run. There was no doubt in my mind that they were thinking about how fat and slow I was. When they cheered me on they really thought I was pathetic for taking so long to run and found it funny to provoke me. They all shared this inside joke while they watched me struggle to finish running my laps.

That theory ended up leaving me extremely depressed. Everyone was silently making fun of me while I ran, and there was nothing I could do about it. And the fact that I had finished among the last in the group only seemed to validate one of my biggest insecurities: I was fat. Or at least fatter than anyone else in my class. If I couldn't finish running a mile at the same time as the majority of the class, obviously I wasn't as fit as everyone else.

Following that mile, I was bombarded with constant thoughts of how disgusting my body was. I felt inferior to my classmates because I couldn't finish the mile at the same time as them, and I always found a way to remind myself that everyone was silently making fun of me.

It was like every one of my inner alarms went off. Anxiety, social anxiety, and depression all in one. Running gave me anxiety. Running in front of other people gave me social anxiety. And being reminded of how out of shape I was triggered major depression.

I had hoped that this adverse reaction to hearing that we were going to run the mile was a one-time thing. Unfortunately, I was way off. The next time we were going to run the mile, my coach announced it a week in advance, and I immediately shut down. I was so anxious about running it– and having other people watch me do it.

Depression took approximately five minutes to set in. If I was more fit then I would be able to run it faster, and we wouldn't be having this problem. Maybe if I wasn't such a fattie I'd be able to run it in under ten minutes.

For the next three days, I was a complete ball of anxiety and stress. On top of all of my other schoolwork now I also had to worry about the impending mile and embarrassing myself in front of the rest of my class. I could be having the best time with my friends, talking about God knows what. And suddenly, I would remember that I would have to run the mile in three days. And I would become so depressed and anxious about it that it was all I could think about. I obsessed over my predicament; the anticipation of the mile literally threatened to break me.

I know it sounds dumb to get so worked up about something as small as running a mile during class. I couldn't really explain why it had this effect on me, why I had so much anxiety about running in general, or why I so strongly hated the idea of other people seeing me run.

But for the next three mile-runs, I was sent back to this dark place every time. All day, every day I obsessed over why I wasn't good enough because I couldn't run the mile. I constantly told myself how horrible it would be, other people watching me and cheering me on like I wasn't privy to their inside jokes about my shortcomings and pathetic athletic abilities.

And this happened every. single. time. As soon as the coach announced that we would be running the mile in a few days, my day and the rest of my entire week was ruined. If she announced on Friday that we would be running it the following Tuesday, my weekend might as well have not existed, because there was no way I was having any fun or relaxation now.

Just hearing my coach talk about when the mile would take place almost sent me into a full-blown panic attack, and each time I had to find a way to make sure no one knew that I was freaking out on the inside. At this point, I was pretty experienced in keeping my panic/anxiety off of my face, so while everyone made jokes about how much they hated the mile and complained about having to run it, I played along, trying to look as nonchalant as they were, even though I was screaming internally.

Yet my panic somehow wasn't the biggest issue that arose at times like that. Every time the date of the mile would be announced I found myself wanting to cut.

I needed an outlet. I needed some way to get the anxiety and depression out. I felt like I was literally under pressure, and I thought cutting would be a good way to get it out. I wanted a break from emotional conflict and figured I could substitute physical pain. I was desperate. I needed *something*. Something had to change or else I was going to hurt myself.

One weekend, during the middle of the quarter when we didn't have to run the mile, I decided I had had enough. Even the time when I didn't have to run the mile I still obsessed over how I would just have to run it again and sank lower into depression. I told my mom that I was having issues with running the mile, because I didn't like other people looking at me while doing it, and it left me depressed whenever I thought about it. This was all completely true, but I didn't want to tell her the whole story– I felt it was best to keep the details minimal. She convinced me to go talk to my P.E. coach and ask if there was an alternative for running the mile.

And there was… kind of. The mile runs made up about half of our final grade in P.E., and for those who were physically unable to run the mile, their assignment was to write a paper on a topic of the coach's choice. When they were finished, they would turn it into the teacher, and they would use the grade of the paper instead of the grade of the mile they couldn't run.

I felt like this was a pretty fair trade, but just in case my coach wasn't okay with me writing the paper and thought I was just trying to get out of running the mile, I also decided that maybe I could still run the mile. I would just do it on the elliptical instead of on the track.

The anxiety was still there, regardless of where I ran, but it was a hair less if I ran on the elliptical. No one except a P.E. teacher would be watching me run, and that would take away some of the social anxiety. Running on the elliptical alone would also take away some of the depression that went with always finishing last or close to last. And thinking about running on the elliptical didn't make me nearly as anxious as running it on the track, because I knew I could handle it– we had an elliptical at home. It wasn't a lot, but it was better than what I had been doing.

So, I worked up the courage to talk to my P.E. coach and explained my situation to her. I told her about how running gave be a lot of anxiety and running in front of other people gave me crazy social anxiety. (I left out the part about the depression– I didn't want them to write home to my mom or something.)

I told her that I was able to write the paper as a substitute for running the mile and that if she didn't feel like that was enough, I was also willing to meet her halfway and run on the elliptical, so I wouldn't get so anxious. I think she thought I was crazy, because running is usually a stress reliever, but it had the complete opposite effect on me. Regardless, she listened and told me she would get back to me about it.

That was all I could ask for. I really just needed someone to hear me and at least try to understand what I was going through. I knew it all sounded crazy, but I guess sometimes mental health doesn't make much sense. I needed some kind of compromise, because my anxiety about running the mile was taking a huge toll. I didn't know what I would do to myself if I had to run the miles on the track in front of the rest of the class again. And I didn't want to find out.

Later in the week, I got a pass for a meeting with my guidance counselor and walked up to her office at the allotted time. These meetings were usually just thirty second check-in sessions that the counselors call students for randomly throughout the year, so I tried to prepare my answers for questions about friends and college plans (or lack thereof).

When I made it up to her office I walked in, and she greeted me, asking me to take a seat. I had made a mental list of all of my classes from favorite to least favorite, and I was ready for any question she would throw my way.

She looked at me and told me that she had talked to my P.E. coach about my "situation." I wasn't ready for that. I had wanted that conversation to stay between the coach and me; I didn't feel like anyone else needed to be involved. The coach could give me her answer, and we could make it work without other people knowing.

Emphasis on the whole "other people won't know" part. I felt betrayed that my coach had spoken to someone else about my situation– none of my classmates knew about it and I didn't want any of the other teachers to know about it. It was already embarrassing to be the kid who had trouble doing something as simple as running the mile, and I'm sure most of the other teachers would have simply assumed I was just too lazy to run it. I felt ridiculous and pathetic enough just talking to my coach about it, and now, apparently other people knew too.

Her words knocked me off balance, and I felt myself go completely pale. Ever since that incident sophomore year when I told my school counselor that I had OCD and she said, "don't we all?" I'd made a point to keep my problems away from the guidance department. But now, here I was, sitting in my counselor's office, about to hear her try to tell me that they were "very experienced" in dealing with mental illness and anxiety.

I braced myself and tried to slow my breathing as she went on to tell me that, like my P.E. coach had said, the only way I would be able to write the paper instead of running the mile was if I was physically hurt. Since I was physically fine, I would have to continue to run the mile. She didn't even bring up running on the elliptical instead.

I couldn't breathe. Just because she couldn't see it meant that it wasn't real? Was my mental illness different from a physical ailment purely because it was mental? How many times would I have to endure people telling me that what was happening on the inside wasn't valid because it was in my head? My eyes stung. Did people think that mental illnesses weren't as debilitating as physical ailments? I had ten years and counting of painful memories of my anxiety and OCD to disprove that.

Before I even left my guidance counselor's office, I could feel my depression rising inside me. Obviously, no one understood what I was going through. If I couldn't even get my guidance counselor, the person who is supposed to help you not have a breakdown, to understand, then no one would.

I walked into the stairwell and stood there, not knowing what to do. I was about to start sobbing, but there was nowhere for me to go if I did that. If someone saw me crying, they would bring me back to the counselor who had just finished telling me that she couldn't make any accommodations for the sake of my mental health. So all I could do was stand there and wait for myself to calm down. I wouldn't let myself cry. Everyone else would know when I walked back into class and would want me to tell them what happened. That wasn't an option.

I stayed in the stairwell for a good five minutes, trying my best to remember what my therapists had said about deep breathing. Thank God no one walked in for those few minutes, because if I was looking half as bad as I was feeling, I probably looked like I was about to go to the roof and jump off. When I finally trusted myself to not lose it upon seeing another student, I returned to class, and acted like nothing had ever happened.

When I got home, I finally allowed myself to shed the tears I had been holding in all day. I hated this. I knew my fear of the mile was stupid, and that was part of the reason it upset me so much. Why did I have to have anxiety in the first place? Why did I have to be so pathetically unathletic that I couldn't run the mile in the same amount of time as everybody else? Why did my coach bring my guidance counselor into it when she could have just left the situation between us? And did I need to remind myself how pathetic I was?

I wanted to cut. I needed a way for all the pressure to come out. My *guidance counselor* didn't even understand. My school thought they were extremely aware and diligent when it came to mental health, but obviously they didn't care as much as they led everyone to believe. That was one of the things that got me the most.

I'd continued seeing Dr. C throughout the summer before junior year, and at the beginning of the school year, she brought in another psychologist who specialized in OCD to help her out. Dr. C didn't feel like we were making any progress– and we weren't. I'd stalled every attempt for her to come to my house and do an exposure, and for the most part, our sessions were just us talking about my life. My depression wasn't getting any better and neither was my anxiety.

So, I began seeing Dr. F instead. She put a big emphasis on finding something to do that I looked forward to every day. She knew I was depressed, (I don't think I did a very good job of hiding that at therapy) and we thought of things I liked doing. After finishing homework every night, I would dedicate some time to that activity in an attempt to add some excitement to the hell that was high school.

She brought me fliers for activities in the community so I could get out of the house and printed articles for me to read about stress relief. She emailed me links to websites made specifically to calm you down during a panic attack, and she made me do some exposures involving my social anxiety. At first it seemed like I was going to start making lots of progress, but eventually it all came to a halt.

I had never been forthcoming with information during therapy, regardless of which therapist I was seeing. I've always preferred to keep emotions and anxiety and stuff to myself. They had to pry it out of me, making for a painful therapy session that I dreaded every week. As soon as we would get to the office I would shut down. No emotion, no motivation, no hope. In fact, during the session, more often than not, I would unknowingly dissociate, only half comprehending what was being said.

We tried to make progress on the social anxiety front, because it was the easiest to pinpoint and provided an opportunity for lots of exposures. But by the time junior year ended, I was over it. We weren't making any real progress, and I dreaded my appointments every week. I felt like it was just a big waste of time—just like all of my other failed therapy attempts.

Eventually, one day when I was alone in the car with my mom, I strategically brought it up. I knew that if I told her that I didn't plan on ever going back to therapy she would have refused, so I told her that I just wanted a break. I didn't feel like I was making any progress and I didn't want to keep wasting money on something I wasn't getting anything out of (which was true).

She agreed to let me take a break and encouraged me to consider looking for another therapist to start seeing instead. I refused. I had seen too many therapists too many times and had gotten nowhere near enough results. I was done with therapy.

Chapter 15

Senior Year: It's Better If You Do

That summer was pretty ordinary. I rotated mostly between work and home, going out with friends occasionally. I was still depressed, but there were plenty of times when I found myself almost giddy thinking about how junior year was over and I could do what I wanted with my summer. The thought was absolutely beautiful. I didn't have to wake up early in the morning then go straight to my silent prison where everyone thought I was weird for the next two months. I was content.

But every time things started going really well and I started feeling really happy, I would remember that I had to go back to school. And when I got back to school I would have to go back to not talking, and even worse than that, I would have to run eight more miles. The cycle would start all over again– announcement of the impending mile, ridiculous amounts of depression and anxiety, thoughts about self-harm and suicide, and the unavoidable fact that my P.E. coach wouldn't understand my predicament just like my coach from junior year.

Those thoughts immediately sent me into a depressive episode that would last anywhere between a few hours to a few days. I hated myself more than ever, especially because I couldn't find the motivation to start working out. Depression took away my motivation to do pretty much anything physical, and if there were any other reasons why I wanted to work out, my anxiety made them unimportant.

Social anxiety made the gym completely out of the question, and I couldn't even stand to work out alone, because I disgusted myself so much. One look at myself in the mirror and all of my insecurities came back. I was stuck in this cycle of feeling really good about my summer, remembering school and the mile, and plunging into a fit of depression.

About halfway through the summer, I decided that I couldn't live like this anymore. The school year hadn't even started, and I was already so anxious about the mile that I felt like I needed to cut myself to get rid of some tension. I knew that I wouldn't be able to handle it when I went back to school. I decided to talk to my new P.E. coach about my situation, not so much because I wanted to go through that process again, but because I needed to. I didn't know what I would do if I had to go through what the mile had put me through last year. If I couldn't even handle the thought of it during the summer, how would I be able to handle actually running it during the school year?

I knew I ran the risk of the exact same thing as last year happening to me again, but I really didn't feel like I had a choice.

Maybe the new coach would understand? I made sure not to get my hopes up; I was well aware of the fact that my anxiety over such a trivial-seeming subject came across as farfetched and dumb to other people. I did everything in my power to expect nothing to change, but as hard as I tried, I still couldn't help but have a little bit of hope that my new P.E. coach would understand.

When school let back in, I waited as long as possible to have the actual conversation with my P.E. teacher. And eventually one day when there was some down time, I decided I might as well get it over with. I'd had to keep my hopes low for too long, and I was started to actually think that my coach would be on my side.

So, I asked my coach if I could talk to her on the down low, and at the end of class I explained my situation, shaking so badly that I couldn't stand up straight. I told her about how the mile gave me anxiety for a reason that was unknown even to me, and just talking about it sent me to the edge of a panic attack. I told her that running in front of other people gave me social anxiety that I couldn't shake. And I told her that the thought of the mile was enough to make me depressed for weeks, because I was forced to confront both my anxiety and my physical insecurities. I asked her to accept one of the two compromises I had offered last year: writing the paper or running on the elliptical. Maybe even both. The entire conversation came out in what probably sounded like one long word, but I had said what I needed to, and I could finally breathe.

I stood there waiting for her to say that she would think about it or just tell me "no" on the spot. But instead, what she did really surprised me. She explained that, as a P.E. coach, her job was to keep the students active. For that reason, she didn't want me to write the paper, but would instead allow me to run the mile on the elliptical.

I was more than happy with that. Those words immediately lifted five hundred pounds off my shoulders, and for the first time since sophomore year, I had hope for the coming school year. I knew I would still have anxiety about running the mile, even though it would be on the elliptical, but it was small potatoes compared to what I had gone through the previous year.

I was so relieved and grateful that a teacher had finally heard what was going on and had done something to help, instead of acting like I had never had a conversation with them. It was the first time since the beginning of junior year that I could devote myself to obsessing and worrying about something other than running the mile. Now, I could focus on talking in the school building or applying to college or working my way out of my depression.

My coach's answer to the question that had been plaguing me all summer gave me a hope that maybe I could make positive changes to behaviors that I previously had thought were impossible to alter. I set my sights high, determining that talking in the school building would be the first issue I would tackle.

I knew the issue would be motivating myself enough to talk in the school building, because I had become secure and content in my silence. It was familiar, and I thought it was what had gotten me this far. But I knew it wasn't healthy. My coping mechanisms had taken over my life.

I reminded myself how much of my high school experience had been taken away from me because I couldn't have conversations like all of my classmates. This was my *senior* year. Did I really want to spend it in silence and continue to have the rest of the student body think I was mute?

I knew that what I really wanted was to be able to contribute to discussions and get to know the people I had gone to school with for four years. I wanted them to know the real me, not the me that didn't have a personality because I didn't speak. I wanted to be able to raise my hand and ask a question instead of pretending I automatically understood everything, and I wanted to be able to interact with people in class, both classmates and teachers.

I told myself I had pulled it off seventh grade year, my last year in elementary school; I should be able to do the same thing my last year of high school. I wanted to go out with a bang. I didn't want everyone to remember me as the weird, quiet girl that never said anything in the school building but was really funny and normal outside of school. Because I would get that all the time. Whenever I had a conversation with a classmate outside of the school building they always said something about how they didn't realize how funny I was or that they didn't even know what my voice sounded like. I was tired of it.

I was going to talk in the school building senior year– I was determined to do it. And I did.

Every single day I made a point to speak at least once every hour, and with every passing day it got easier. At first, it was actually like pulling teeth. I had to consciously force myself to talk even though every voice in my head was yelling at me to pull myself together. I knew better than this; I couldn't do this to myself. Every hour it usually took me a good while to even hype myself up enough to go through with it.

But eventually, it started to get easier. It felt more natural and less forced, which was exactly what I wanted. I didn't have to think about it as much and got more comfortable with my peers. And all of my classmates seemed to have the same thing to say about my new-found words: "this is the first time I've ever heard you talk!" I can't even count how many times I heard that, and to be honest, it hurt a little bit. It was sad that so many people had never heard me say anything, and it made me mad that I had allowed OCD to keep me quiet for so long. But every time I had to laugh those words off it was a reminder of what I'd been through, and it just made me more motivated to talk.

The more I got into the groove, the more I regretted not doing this sooner; I felt like I had wasted so much time. But talking in the school building had seemed impossible to be done any sooner. I guess I had to do it on my time and on my terms. That was one of the hardest tasks I've ever pulled off in my life, but the reward was very well worth it.

That year without a therapist I made some of the most progress I had made in years. I knew I still had a long way to go, but I learned things about my anxiety and depression that I could only hope would help me in the long run.

And on graduation day when I walked across that stage there was only one thought in my head: I made it. I made it through high school with good grades throughout all five years while fighting with my brain every single day. I made it through high school without any of my classmates knowing about my anxiety, OCD, or depression. I made it through without my friends ever knowing that I was suicidal and without ever having to tell anyone at school (besides my PE teachers) about my issues. I had gotten to leave that part of my life private, just the way I wanted it.

The biggest thing, though, was just that I had made it through high school. There were times when I genuinely didn't know if I would make it to graduation day. If you had told me sophomore year that I would still be alive to graduate I wouldn't have believed it. There were so many days that I couldn't imagine living to see tomorrow, and I definitely couldn't imagine myself living to graduate high school.

There are some moments in your life when you take a step back and think to yourself how grateful you are that you didn't kill yourself that time you thought it was the only option. For me, my high school graduation was one of them. I was actually proud of myself for getting to where I was, that I managed to hang in there even when it seemed impossible.

The last three years I had stayed alive pretty much because I didn't want my family to have to go through the experience of a loved one committing suicide. And there I was– not only alive, but actually hopeful for the future. I couldn't remember the last time I had felt that way, and I hoped it wouldn't be the last.

Chapter 16

Here and Now

Now I'm going to college, and I'm trying really hard to look at this next step of my life as an opportunity to make progress in my mental health. I've learned a lot about myself in the years since I was first diagnosed with PANDAS when I was six, and I've learned a lot about the rest of the world. I know now that I can't always assume that other people will know what I'm going through. I can't ever make anyone else understand. I'm hoping that it's enough that I might be starting to understand myself.

I've realized that my anxiety and OCD don't necessarily revolve solely around vomiting anymore. The smallest things cause me anxiety, even if it doesn't pose the threat of getting sick. In any given situation, no matter how harmless it may seem, my anxiety weeds out the worst-case scenario, and my OCD takes that situation and obsesses over it. It runs through my head in vivid detail. What if this happens? What if this happens but in a totally unrealistic way that only anxiety would be able to come up with?

Even though the vast majority of my anxiety still has to do with vomiting, I continue to struggle a lot with the small things. Now I know that when I start having those kinds of thoughts, I have to find a way to calm myself down or else a panic attack will ensue. And I'm hoping that by being conscious of my thoughts and how worked up I'm getting over them, I'll be able to prevent future panic attacks.

Unfortunately, I still don't know most of my triggers for panic attacks, but I know what one feels like, and I guess that has to be enough. It's certainly better than the absolutely nothing I knew before. When I get a panic attack, my thoughts speed up so fast that it actually feels like they're running around in circles in my head. I have a hard time focusing on anything other than the anxious thoughts, and I start to feel like I can't breathe. I get nauseous and don't want to move because it feels like my thoughts are already moving at the speed of light. My heart starts beating really fast, and I shake uncontrollably.

Usually, I can feel a panic attack coming on, but sometimes they happen out of the blue. Admittedly, I'm not good at talking myself through the anxiety like therapists say to do and usually have to settle for distracting myself as best as possible until I feel better. It's not the ideal coping method, but I just do what I can.

My depression has been manageable for the most part, but albeit still very much there. Sometimes I find myself in a place that depression medication can't even reach. I've started to notice myself going into depressive episodes sporadically, a new development that I'm trying to make sense of. I call them "depression attacks," because they come on unexpectedly and can last anywhere from a few hours to a few days. The smallest thing can trigger a depression attack, and once the depression's there, it's impossible to stop it.

The severity of each attack varies depending on the circumstances. Sometimes it gets so bad that I cry despite my best efforts not to, and sometimes I just get really grumpy. Without fail, though, every time I have a depression attack, I feel the need to cut myself and have to consciously talk myself out of it. I'm hoping that the urge to cut doesn't get worse than it already is, and I especially hope that I won't give into it.

So far, my go-to coping mechanism when I have a depression attack is distancing myself from the rest of my family as subtly as possible (none of them know about the depression attacks) and stay that way for as long as I need to feel back to normal.

My OCD has also left me with many ways to make sure I never forget that it's there.
Besides the rituals and protective measures I have to go through on a daily basis, I also have a tic that's been with me for the majority of the years following my diagnosis. It's a neck stretch that I do… I feel like I have to do. Depending on my stress level, I get the urge to

stretch my neck sporadically throughout the day. On days when I'm more stressed than others, I feel the need to stretch my neck more; when I'm having a good day I do it less. If I don't do it, the urge just gets stronger until I let the tic happen. On average, I probably get the urge to stretch my neck about once every five to ten minutes. On bad days it can increase to once every one to two minutes.

At first, I didn't really mind the tic, but it didn't take very long for it to get in the way of my daily activities. Whenever I get the urge to stretch my neck, I have to stop immediately to do it. Sometimes I'll be in the middle of talking, sometimes in the middle of singing a song, sometimes hanging out with friends, or sometimes while I'm at work. I'll be in the middle of telling a story and have to stop to perform the tic while everyone else waits for me to finish what I was saying. It's embarrassing.

Everywhere I go, the tic comes with me, no matter how much I try to stifle it. I know other people notice it– it's not exactly subtle. On several separate occasions I have done it while I was at school and one of my classmates made a comment or laughed because I was "dancing." When I'm at work, I try to do it without my coworkers noticing, and no matter how hard I try I know they do. They've asked me many times what I was doing with my neck, and I've just laughed it off, making up the excuse that I had a crick in my neck or something.

I've also noticed another weird symptom that I've had for as long as I can remember: my hands shake twenty-four/seven. I don't know if it has to do with my medicine I'm on to help with my OCD and anxiety, but my hands shake uncontrollably every second of every day. There's always a constant tremor, but sometimes it's worse than others. When I'm especially anxious or my blood sugar is low, I start shaking so badly that I have trouble holding things.

I actually grew up thinking that that's what happened to everyone. I thought everyone's hands shook at all times, so I didn't even realize it was out of the ordinary. But when other people started taking notice, I did too. I would be having a regular conversation at work, and my coworker would suddenly point out that I was shaking. They would ask if there was something wrong or if I was nervous. I wasn't. It was just a normal conversation.

Then my friends at school started noticing and asked if everything was okay. I took the opportunity to ask them if they shake all the time as well, because it had started to don on me that maybe shaking twenty-four/seven wasn't normal. They informed me that, no, people's hands aren't supposed to shake like that. Ever since then, I've been very aware of how much I shake and how others may interpret it.

Every time a classmate asks me to hand them something I watch as my hand shakes and anticipate the usual questions of if I'm feeling okay. I always just tell everyone that I'm fine, I always shake, and hope they drop the subject. Some of my teachers worriedly comment on how much my hands are shaking when I turn in my essays, and I have to make up a phony excuse about it. One night at work, I was painfully aware of how it looked like I was nervous about training the new guy at work because of how much my hands were shaking when I handed him a receipt. I wasn't nervous. I just always shake.

At first, I thought the shaking was just another harmless side effect, until I realized I couldn't write like a normal person because I was shaking so much. I had to reteach myself how to write while adapting to my shaking that occasionally got so bad that I could barely hold a pen.

So maybe the shaking isn't as harmless as I had originally thought. It kind of sucks, actually. I know that other people notice, and it doesn't help my social anxiety to think about what they think of me for shaking so much. I know that every time I take a picture, I have to take at least ten because nine of them will be blurry. And I know that people notice my tic, whether they think I'm dancing or trying to fix a crick in my neck. It makes the social anxiety worse, but it's something I'll have to deal with.

When everything is said and done, I can't help but realize how lucky I am to have the support system I did and still do. I know that I'm extremely fortunate to have people around me that try so hard to get me the help I need. And I'm very much aware that this is not the reality for a lot of people out there struggling with mental illness. So many people have similar issues to what I've gone through and have less support from the people around them. Hell, even with my support system, I still struggle with suicidal thoughts. I can't imagine having to go through it completely alone.

That's one of the reasons I wrote this book. I need people who aren't struggling with mental illness to know that even if you can't see what's going on inside someone's head, it's still just as real and as serious as a physical injury. If someone around you is having a hard time fighting their demons, don't try to tell them that it's not real or that they need to shake it off. That's not how it works, and that will most likely result in the person who is struggling thinking that there is something wrong with them. That's the kind of thing that leads to depression and suicide. Because believing that they should be able to magically cure what's going on inside their head is what makes people isolate themselves— that's what makes them not want help.

I need people to know that mental illness is very much a real issue. If it wasn't real, why would someone opt to live their life the way a person with a mental disorder does? It's not cool, and it doesn't get you sympathy points. It's inconvenient, and it's definitely not any fun. It sucks. It really, really sucks. So, please don't accuse someone of exaggerating their anxiety when they're in the middle of an anxiety attack. And please don't tell someone who is depressed that they need to just brighten up. If it were like that, life would be a million times easier. They're not trying to gain your sympathy or make excuses. It's real, and a lot of people would give anything to live their lives like normal people.

If you are currently struggling with a mental illness, you aren't alone. I know what it's like to feel hopeless in your situation, and I know how hard it is to figure out a way to make life work. This is just a reminder that the fact that you've made it this far is a clear indicator of how strong you are. There is no doubt in my mind that the things that you have to put up with every day are shaping you into the person you are, and you should be proud of how much you've accomplished. It might not seem like it, but every day is a victory. I've learned that from all these years of feeling like I wasn't making any progress in my recovery. Know that even the smallest things make a difference.

As for me, I know that I'm going to struggle with my OCD, anxiety, and depression every single day for the rest of my life. There will be good days and bad days; there will be many more times when I think about just ending it. But it's made me into the person I am today; everything I've gone through has taught me a lesson that is essential to who I am as a person.

All of my years of silence have taught me to listen, and all my years of trying to control my life have showed me that I can't always be in control. All of those hours spent in therapy weren't for nothing– they helped me on my continuing journey to recovery. All of the hurtful things people had said to me over the years made me learn to never judge anyone prematurely for their behaviors or habits– I don't know what's going on inside their head. And all of those times I cried alone in my bed and felt like I wanted to end things weren't for nothing either– getting through those nights has taught me that I'm stronger than I thought I was. At the darkest times when I didn't feel strong enough to get through, somehow, I did. So now when the darkness comes back, I can remind myself that I can get through it. I've done it once and I can do it again.

So, I know that my future holds more anxiety and panic attacks and suicidal thoughts. That's something I'm going to have to fight against every day. I've come a long way, but I still have a long way to go. But for the first time in a long time, I'm hopeful for the future, and that's way more than I could have said a year ago. I guess I'm just going to have to wait and see what the future holds. And keep working tirelessly on my anxiety, depression, OCD, and me.

A Note From the Author

I wrote this book in high school with the hopes of getting it published to not only spread mental health awareness, but to also remind people struggling with mental illness that they are not alone. There were many times throughout my journey that I felt lonely in my experiences. I wanted to write this book to share my story so that maybe someone reading can relate to some of these experiences and feel less alone in their journey. If just one person benefits from reading about my experiences that is enough.

I went back and forth for a while trying to decide if I did actually want to share some of my most private memories and thoughts. A big factor that played into my decision to publish this book was thinking about if reading a book like this would have helped me when I was feeling my most alone and defeated when I was in elementary school or high school. I think it would have.

On a different note, I want to encourage anyone who is feeling helpless or lost to seek help. At my lowest points I did not want to ask for help, but in reality, that is what I needed the most. And let this serve as a reminder that coping mechanisms, medications, therapy treatments, etc. are not one size fits all. What helps your friend may not help you. You are not broken for not reacting to something the same way someone else does. You just need to try something different.

I hope that someone finds my story helpful. Mental health is a slippery slope that is very unforgiving, but we are not alone in this fight. There are people around us who can help when the future seems bleak. In the meantime, take it one day at a time. You've got this.